ECHL 2 NHL

ECHL 2 NHL

DEVELOPING NHL PLAYERS

GRIFFIN PHILLIPS
GERMOND

NEW DEGREE PRESS

Photography as seen on the cover by Michael Cox.

ECHL 2 NHL

Developing NHL Players

ISBN   978-1-64137-327-2   *Paperback*

             978-1-64137-634-1   *Ebook*

CONTENTS

ACKNOWLEDGEMENTS

A special thank-you to the following people for funding the Indiegogo campaign that allowed me to successfully publish this book:

Adam Goldberg

Adam Peterson

Adam Tuchinsky

Alexa Zurek

Alexander Benson

Alexander Booker

Alexandra Congel

Alexis Gillis

Amanda Colaneri

Amanda S. Germond

Amanda Spink

Andrew Margison

Anton Gulovsen

Ashley Dubrasich

Avery Germond

Ben Cherry

Ben Daigle

Brian Johnson

Bryson Wrobel

Cassandra Thompson

Chip Brewer

Chris Salamone

Clement T. Madden

Cynthia H. Madden

David Bantz

David Savidge

Dennis Gilbert

Diane Vail

Doug & Doger Gilliland

Dulcie H. Germond

Elisabeth Maxfield

Elise Fisher

Elizabeth A. Germond

Elizabeth Rogers

Eric Koester

Eric Smith

Evan Johnson

Gene St. Cyr

Isabelle Wareham

Jacqueline Amico

Jake Collupy

Jamison Lane

Jeanette Andonian

Jedidiah Taft

Jeffrey W. Gillis

Jennifer Regen Boch

Jill Heintz

Jordanne Henault

Joseph Colaneri

Joshua Perry

Josh Plowman

Justin Broy

Katie Lambert

Kayla Caulfield

Kevin Hopkins

Kieran Joyce

Kristen Stoddard

Lars Sjulander

Leonard Shedletsky

Lilia Madden

Lindsey Madden

Linsey MacDougall

Lisa Bird

Marianne Stoddard

Mario Perry

Mark DeShong

Mary Adams

Mary Guimond

Mary McCrann

Matt Roy

Matthew Buotte

Michael Chapin

Michael S. Washington

Morgan Brear

Nancy Hurst

Nate Harvey

Nathaniel Germond	Scott Stroh
Nathaniel Payne	Steven Smith
Paul Riley	Suzanne Phillips
Rebecca Nisetich	Teddy Germond
Ricky Milliner	Terence Phillips
Ryan Chesley	Thomas Lipoma
Ryan Gaudreau	Tommy Dahlborg
Sam Tracy	Tyler Durkee
Samantha Nichols	Wayne Dyment
Scott Cook	Win Gillis
Scott Engelter	Winthrop C. Gillis

Thank you to the following people for interviews and creating content within the book itself:

Connor LaCouvee	Josh Currie
David Farrar	Riley Armstrong
Jacob MacDonald	Shane Harper

Thank you to Darryl Dionne and the Professional Hockey Players' Association for helping me with interviewing processes, and sparking new ideas!

Thank you to Maine-based photographer Michael Cox for allowing me to use his photography for my cover.

Thank you to the Elite Prospects team for their statistical database of hockey players and teams. It is the best statistical hockey database in the world.

Lastly, thank you to Eric Koester, Brian Bies, Kim LaCoste, Russell Kivatisky, and New Degree Press for their continued support and assistance throughout this journey. You never doubted my ability to write this, even when I did. Thank you for pushing me and never throwing in the towel.

PREFACE

———

Ever since I can remember, hockey has been an integral part of my life. My earliest memories include flipping through 1999–00 Upper Deck MVP hockey cards on the couch with my dad. We lived only about thirty minutes away from Phillips Arena, home of the now-defunct Atlanta Thrashers. Every game that my uncle went to, he'd bring me back a souvenir. The Thrashers' signature "puck hat," still hangs on my bedpost. Bobbleheads still line the top of my dresser.

When my family began to shift their lifestyle and move to Maine—the polar opposite of a place like Georgia—it was apparent to both me and my father that I would be playing hockey.

And so, at five years old, I completed my first "learn-to-skate" in Brunswick, Maine, at Bowdoin College. I was hooked.

* * *

The Southeast isn't exactly a hockey hotbed, for the most part. There are exceptions to that. Such as, the Carolina Hurricanes, Tampa Bay Lightning... and you could make the argument for the Florida Panthers, but their attendance numbers are just really hard to look at for a major league professional sports team. And, at the time that I moved, the Atlanta Thrashers, too.

But, down south, unlike life here in Maine, there aren't hockey rinks every twenty to thirty minutes inland. In fact, other than Phillips Arena in downtown Atlanta, there wasn't a hockey rink within an hour of us.

Whether my dad wants to admit it or not, I know that there was a hidden motive in moving to the north: To give me the opportunity to play the game that he loved so much as a kid, and still does to this day.

Once we moved to Maine, collectively, we settled in the small town of Gorham. Lucky for us, there was a rink only a three-minute drive away from our house, due west at the University of Southern Maine—a college that I am now a proud alumnus of. The beach was twenty minutes east, and so was Maine's largest city, Portland—which has another smaller rink, of course. Truthfully, there were rinks all around us.

And, when the snow comes in the winter, the ponds freeze over, and there are more "rinks."

Portland, notably, also has a rink for their professional team.

To have such a mix of younger players, middle-of-the-road players, college players, professional players, and retired players in the same general vicinity of each other makes a well-rounded hockey culture. And, without it, my love for the game would never have flourished in such a way that it did.

* * *

From 2001 to 2003, my parents owned season tickets to the Portland Pirates, a now-defunct American Hockey League (AHL) team that had a historical past. They became a team when the "old" Maine Mariners left.

In 2002, at just six years old, I began playing ice hockey on teams within the Huskies Youth Hockey Association in Gorham, Maine (now the Southern Maine Youth Hockey Association).

From early on in my hockey career, I remember that Pirates players used to make the twenty minute drive out to Gorham at the University of Southern Maine's ice arena to come shoot around with eager wide-eyed kids like myself, and maybe teach us a thing or two.

Because, at the end of every practice with these guys, we'd line up for autographs and pictures, and they'd happily oblige. My dad would take out his ancient cell phone and hope for a picture that wasn't completely blurred.

Most of the time, we didn't know who these players were. We didn't care. They were prospects of National Hockey League (NHL) teams, and journeyman players looking to extend their playing careers simply for the love of the game.

Growing up, the local players were my heroes.

These minor league hockey players were my heroes.

And, I believe they were heroes for other kids too.

As you can tell, I fell in love with the game at a very early age.

* * *

Years later, looking at autographed pucks, it's hard to make out who's who, and if any signature is worth more than just sentimental value.

But, as a kid, you just didn't care. These were the guys you looked up to. And so, I find these autographed Pirates pucks in bargain bins and garage sales and buy them. Not because they're necessarily worth a whole lot, but they bring about a sense of nostalgia.

Now, this isn't to say those autographed pucks are all worthless. The Portland Pirates helped develop many present and former NHL players, including the likes of Olaf Kolzig, Ryan Getzlaf, Corey Perry, Andrew Brunette, Jordan Martinook, Nathan Gerbe, Tyler Ennis, Sergei Gonchar, Jhonas Enroth... the list goes on, and I left many notable names out.

When the Pirates were affiliated with the Mighty Ducks, and then just Ducks, in the mid-2000s, I was starting to make sense of things. In 2005–06, the Pirates had a star-studded roster that included: Ryan Getzlaf, Corey Perry, Ryan Shannon, Shane O'Brien, Zenon Konopka, P.A. Parenteau, Dustin Penner, Curtis Glencross, Ladislav Smid, and even Bobby Ryan (for the playoffs at least).

While each of these players played for varying amounts of time throughout the season, being able to go to a game on any given night and see future NHL talent play right before my eyes was pretty neat, especially being a young hockey player. It got me hooked. When they got called up, I made sure to see it. My dad and I would stay up late past my 9:00 p.m. bedtime and watch a Pacific west-coast Ducks game that saw so many familiar faces that were on the Pirates.

The point being, watching the future of the game develop before my eyes was something that really sparked my love for the sport of ice hockey.

So, naturally, in 2016 when it was announced that the Portland Pirates were up for sale and most likely going to be relocated, I remember exactly where I was at that time. I was sitting in the television room in my house, my heart racing, and eyes tearing up. I pulled your prototypical espresso-infused collegiate all-nighter, only instead of studying, I was starting a petition to keep them in Portland. It received over 500 signatures. I was interviewed for a hockey article. I was even on my local news for a short time. I had people signing from all over the country—and even from international locations. It was beautiful to see so many people express their love for a minor league hockey team.

Then, within what seemed like minutes, the Portland Pirates closed their doors and moved on to Springfield, the home of the AHL headquarters. I distinctly remember so many players being distraught. Shane Harper voiced his discontent to my buddy at his workplace. Mike McKenna was saddened to be moving away.

For two years, the Cross Insurance Arena in downtown Portland was vacant. Sure, there was the occasional country concert or college hockey game, but the loss of minor league hockey just made the arena look like a ghost town. It hurt local businesses, and it pained the hockey community in Maine.

A lot of people have this idea that Maine is just minutes from Boston. You go overseas, and you tell people you're from Maine. They look at you funny, and then you soften the awkwardness by saying "close to Boston," and then their eyes light up. I've heard people refer to Maine as part of Canada as well. To be fair, we're pretty close to being that.

The reality for many hockey fans is that we aren't close to Boston. I grew up in more or less a New York sports household, so my team is the Rangers, but more on them in a bit.

Regardless, at the tip of Southern Maine, you're probably still around an hour or so from Boston. A Boston Bruins game is like a once-a-year thing around here, especially if you're a hockey-playing kid that travels on the weekends, and whose week is engulfed in homework. That was me.

And, let's not forget the cost incurred in going to a Bruins game. The price of a soda and a hot dog for four people is as much as a family four pack at your local minor league hockey game. And heck, if you're planning on sitting anywhere other than in the balcony for a family of four at TD Garden, or the

FleetCenter as it used to be called, you'd be spending the same amount as it costs for a season seat for three quarters of a season at—you guessed it—your local minor league hockey team.

So, when the Pirates did leave, kids didn't really have those local guys to look up to anymore. Getting to a major professional hockey game was more of a pain than it was a convenience—for parents, I should add.

You never know what you have until it's gone, as they say.

* * *

In 2017, though, it was announced that we'd be seeing a team back in Maine. Something we hadn't seen before, an East Coast Hockey League (ECHL) team. They became affiliated with the Rangers, and in early 2018, after getting out of class at the University of Southern Maine, I went right on down to the arena and got my single season ticket for the year.

You can imagine my joyous excitement after I learned the affiliation was with my favorite team!

The Maine Mariners of the ECHL made their debut last October, in 2018, losing to the Adirondack Thunder, 6–3. As the season progressed, we had former OHL standout Brandon Halverson become the starting goalie for the team, while also seeing Sean Day who once had OHL Exceptional Player Status drop down for a few games, as well as Rangers seventh round pick from 2016, Ty Ronning, suit up. Halverson had a sparkling season going and was deservedly recalled by the Hartford Wolf Pack just a few days into February. Day only spent.. pardon the pun... days as a Mariners player, as he quite literally looked too good to be playing in the ECHL—and that speaks to how he developed and matured from his first day here to the last day. Ronning, on the other hand, was sent back and forth from the Mariners and Wolf Pack, though on his first night here, he posted three goals and two assists in a come-from-behind 6–4 win.

Hockey was back.

The opportunity for more six-year-olds like I once was to fall in love with the game had returned.

* * *

Professional hockey was met back with warmth by the city of Portland and the surrounding Southern Maine communities. However, being a league lower than the AHL, the general population had questions.

Will I ever see these players make it to the NHL?

Why are the goal posts blue?

Will this level of hockey be sustainable in such a small market?

When the team first started playing, some people drew comparisons of the ECHL to, as one fellow liked to call it, a "Ghetto League."

That is far from the truth.

There were people complaining it wasn't the AHL, it wasn't the same level of hockey, and the players didn't have a future.

The fact of the matter is, the ECHL is a legitimate professional developmental league. By the end of the 2018-19 NHL season, 662 former ECHL players have played in the National Hockey League, and that number is only going to go up.

Take Shane Harper—a former Portland Pirate—worked for years through a plethora of organizations and teams, before finally getting his shot in 2016 with the Florida Panthers.

Or, for instance, Josh Currie, who was a major junior hockey standout with the Prince Edward Island Rocket. He didn't get an NHL contract, he signed an AHL contract, and eventually was sent to the ECHL. But, through perseverance and hard work, Currie played for the Edmonton Oilers this past season, after spending much of his professional career in Bakersfield, California.

Even the once-given OHL Exceptional Status defenseman, Sean Day, played for the Maine Mariners of the ECHL this past year. His confidence skyrocketed from the chances that he was given, earning him an ECHL All-Star game spot. He returned to the AHL before he could play in that game, but his season turned around in the right direction, right away.

While I may not see the star-studded lineup that the 2005–06 Portland Pirates had, I know that on a night-to-night basis, some of these players that I watch in the ECHL will be part of the future of hockey's best league, the NHL.

This is what has sparked my fascination with player development, and why the ECHL deserves more recognition as a true developmental league for NHL-caliber players.

I guess blue goal posts are pretty cool, too.

PART 1

INTRODUCTION

CHAPTER 1

EVERY PLAYER HAS
THEIR STORY

April 26, 2011—Vancouver, BC

The Vancouver Canucks are at home against the Chicago Blackhawks in Game 7 of the NHL's Western Conference quarterfi-
nals. The Blackhawks are coming into the playoffs as the eighth
seed to the Canucks, who finished the season as the number one
team in the conference, as well as earning the President's Trophy
for having the most points in the entire league.

Though the Blackhawks are just one year removed from
winning the Stanley Cup in 2010, they had lost many of the
key pieces from that team, and were coined the "Hangover
Hawks" by many.

This single game means way more than anyone could have ever thought. The Canucks and Blackhawks are meeting in the postseason for the third consecutive year. The previous two years, the Canucks had lost to the Blackhawks, both times in the second round.

This year, based on what happened in the regular season, one would think that the Canucks would cruise over the Blackhawks. But, to this point, the Canucks have won three games to have a 3–0 lead in the series, only to lose the next three games to the Blackhawks, who have clawed for every inch of getting back into this series.

Ultimately, if the Canucks blow this series, they become only the fourth team in NHL history to lose a series after going up 3–0 in a series.

Ouch.

Regardless of what happened in the regular season or in the playoffs the previous two years, this is Game 7. And, if you've taken anything from this past year's 2018–2019 season, it's that anything is possible in this sport.

After all, a team that was first place in the 2018–19 season practically the entire year, the Tampa Bay Lightning, got swept in the first round by a team that many argued had no place even being there. And, to everyone's surprise, the team in last place halfway through the year, the St. Louis Blues, made a miraculous run en route to securing their first Stanley Cup in franchise history.

* * *

Game 7.

Canucks agitator and two-way forward Alex Burrows starts the scoring less than three minutes into the game, off a great individual effort by Ryan Kesler, who dishes the puck to a streaking Burrows right through the middle of the ice.

Rogers Arena goes absolutely nuts.

The game would continue into the third, still 1–0 Canucks, and it looked as if the Canucks were going to "slay the dragon," and move on to the second round, finally defeating the team that had been so costly to their playoff hopes up until this point.

However, with just two minutes remaining, Chicago's captain Jonathan Toews ties the game from his stomach in a second effort in front of the then-much-younger and recently retired goaltender, Roberto Luongo.

The score is tied at one goal apiece before heading into sudden death overtime. Just over five minutes in, Blackhawks defenseman Chris Campoli gathers the puck along the left sideboard in the defensive zone, and attempts to flip the puck up the ice along the boards. This is a pretty standard hockey play.

The flip doesn't go as planned, and Campoli turns the puck over to who else, but Alex Burrows, skating through the Blackhawks' blueline on the forecheck.

The puck is rolling in front of him, and Burrows skates into a slapshot from the top of the hash marks.

The puck zings right past goaltender Corey Crawford's helmet, and right underneath the bar in the top left corner of the net.

The announcers, no matter what station you're listening to or watching the game on, all go wild—except for maybe the Blackhawks radio play-by-play guys, who are less than thrilled. In the heat of the moment, nobody on the Canucks cares about the past two seasons' misfortunes. All that matters is this moment. How they got there is in the past.

The team swarms Burrows, and the Blackhawks are doubled over, writhing in disappointment. It's such a famous moment in Canucks history, and an equally infamous moment in Blackhawks history.

The Canucks would go on to lose to the Boston Bruins in the Stanley Cup Finals. Alex Burrows went on to have a spectacular and somewhat infamous playoff run, notching seventeen points in twenty-five games.

If you know, you know.

* * *

You may be wondering why I've elected to talk about Alex Burrows so much.

In fact, before writing this introduction, or even thinking about writing this book, I had never paid too much attention to Burrows. Especially, back in his NHL rookie season, when he wasn't the most well-known of players. Having collected hockey cards since a young age, I could tell you that his rookie cards were from 2005–06, and that was about it. The 2005–06 rookie class was nothing short of one of the best ever, and Burrows was certainly overshadowed by the likes of Crosby, Ovechkin, Getzlaf, Lundqvist, Perry, and so many more.

He wasn't even the heralded Petr Prucha, who I thought was going to be the epitome of greatness and goal-scoring prowess for my New York Rangers.

Whether you love Burrows or hate him (he'd always been one of "those players" during his playing days), you may not have paid attention to how he actually got into an NHL lineup. He was the guy you loved to have on your team, but hated to play against—at every level.

* * *

If we're being honest, most players aren't like the select few that get drafted and immediately make the NHL lineup straight from their very first training camp.

It's not to say that they didn't earn it, either. They did.

That select group of players, though, pales in comparison to the immense number of players that spend time developing for months to years—whether that be back in their respective junior ranks, college, or the AAA development league of the NHL, the American Hockey League—or, the AHL.

Then, there are those that got their start professionally in the AA developmental league of the NHL, the East Coast Hockey

League—but better known across North America as just the ECHL, ever since 2003, when they ditched four words and went for an easier, more recognizable, and better understood four letters instead.

In fact, Alex Burrows went undrafted. And not only that, his career started in the ECHL.

A player must get an opportunity and run with it to progress from a full-time ECHLer to a full time AHLer to a full time NHLer.

Burrows took these opportunities and ran with them.

A 2017 article by The Vancouver Courier said that:

In retrospect, the biggest moment of his entire hockey career may have been the ECHL contract he signed with the Inferno. The Inferno were the ECHL affiliate of the Manitoba Moose and Vancouver Canucks and Burrows ended up on a line with the Canucks' 9th-round draft pick from 2000, Tim Smith. Burrows helped Smith to the ECHL scoring title and grabbed the attention of Moose general manager Craig Heisinger, signing an AHL contract with the Moose. Two seasons later, he was in the Canucks' lineup.[1]

---

1   "Alex Burrows Was The Unlikeliest Success Story In Canucks History". 2017. Vancouver Courier.

The process of going from the ECHL to the NHL typically isn't something that happens over the same year. It's quite rare that it does—and mostly happens with goaltenders, if it happens at all. Take Brandon Halverson, in 2018, who happened to play in all three leagues, albeit his brief NHL appearance was in relief of Henrik Lundqvist, and his call-up was on an emergency basis. Ken Appleby did the same thing in 2017–18, going from Adirondack, to Binghamton, to New Jersey.

Point being: It's rare.

There have been plenty of "household name" players that got their starts in the ECHL, besides Alex Burrows. Michael Ryder, David Desharnais, Jonathan Quick, Braden Holtby, Mark Streit, and the recently-retired Dan Girardi are just a few. If you want the full list of all ECHL alumni to make it to the NHL, visit the ECHL's website. I would be willing to place it here, if it didn't unnecessarily occupy twenty pages.

We'll stick to a smaller sample.

This past year, in the 2018–19 season, twenty former ECHL players made their NHL debuts:

PLAYER	ECHL TEAM(S)	NHL TEAM	NHL DEBUT
Kaden Fulcher	Toledo	Detroit	April 6
Jake Chelios	Toledo/Kalamazoo	Detroit	March 29
Joshua Jacobs	Adirondack	New Jersey	March 21
Colton White	Adirondack	New Jersey	March 14
Josh Currie	Gwinnett/Bakersfield/ Norfolk	Edmonton	**Feb. 19**
Kole Sherwood	Jacksonville	Columbus	Feb. 16
Kevin Boyle	Utah	Anaheim	Feb. 9
Josh Brown	Manchester	Florida	Jan. 18
Jacob Middleton	Manchester	San Jose	Jan. 5
Marcus Hogberg	Brampton	Ottawa	Dec. 29
Tyler Lewington	South Carolina	Washington	Dec. 22
Mackenzie Blackwood	Adirondack	New Jersey	Dec. 18
Jayce Hawryluk	Manchester	Florida	Dec. 15
Michael Bunting	Rapid City	Arizona	Dec. 11
Eddie Pasquale	Gwinnett/Brampton	Tampa Bay	Dec. 4
Anthony Richard	Cincinnati	Nashville	Dec. 1
Landon Bow	Idaho	Dallas	Nov. 21
Clark Bishop	Florida	Carolina	Oct. 20
Jacob MacDonald	**Elmira/Toledo**	**Florida**	**Oct. 6**
Maxime Lajoie	Brampton	Ottawa	Oct. 4

2

While these players all played varying amounts of time in the
ECHL in their careers, their success was determined by their
ability to take an opportunity and run with it to a higher level.

Just. Like. Burrows.

---

2   "ECHL Alumni". 2019. echl.com. Accessed July 9, 2019.

When those players made their NHL debuts, all that mattered was this moment. How they got there was in the past.

More on the guys that are **bolded**, in just a little bit.

* * *

The ECHL isn't the most widely covered league, and the headlines in the NHL, for the most part, read, "Player X makes NHL debut." There may be a short blurb about the player's time in the ECHL. The same blurb happens if you played five games down there, or 300.

The ECHL also gets a somewhat unfair reputation—as a league that does highlight the entertainment side as a crucial proponent of the games. In fact, some season ticket packages (thirty-six games) around the league cost as much as loge seating for one person at a Boston Bruins versus Montreal Canadiens game. And, the league is known for having a "bash and crash" style of play. "Bash and crash" sells to casual fans and families.

Forty-nine players had one hundred or more penalty minutes this past season.[3]

---

3   "Elite Prospects - ECHL PIM Stats 2018-2019." Elite Prospects, 2019.

You know the kids that go to the games love it. You know that $3 Bud Light nights turn an arena into a social event. It's a night out on the town, for some people, and nothing more. It's this level.

While development is great, it isn't *everything* at this level.

These teams still need to make money.

It is, at the end of everything, still a business, and seats need to be filled.

Being known to develop players is an amazing thing, but the money side is what keeps the players and keeps developing them with great facilities, pay, and solid living conditions.

After attending thirty-nine ECHL games this past year, I've decided to challenge myself and lay it all out there, to write this book. Whether you're a hardcore fan or a casual fan, I hope that you can learn from what you're about to read—or perhaps you've already learned a thing or two after reading the introduction.

The ECHL is undeniably a true developmental league for NHL-caliber players, despite what some may think, or say.

This book aims to shed light on the importance of the ECHL in prospect development for the NHL, including the past, present, and future of the league, while highlighting stories of players that have made it through the ranks of the ECHL to the NHL, and those who are "in the works."

Written by a hockey fan, for hockey fans.

CHAPTER 2

THE THING ABOUT PROSPECT DEVELOPMENT

———

The end goal of prospect development is to develop players that can fill an NHL role on a regular basis, and help a major-league professional team in the long run. Some prospects take very little time to mature into stable NHL players, while others don't see the NHL ice for years, or simply do not pan out at all. It's a fact that not every player is going to turn out like they were "supposed to." Another fact is that some players are going to surprise people and against all odds, be a much better player than those who were supposed to be in their shoes.

One step down from the NHL is the AHL, which is the pre-miere AAA developmental league of the NHL. Players are expected to develop at a faster pace than their AA counter-parts. Some players in the AHL are veterans who bounce between the NHL and AHL on a regular basis—though they're not considered prospects. They're considered depth players, who can fill a role on a team if given the opportu-nity. In many ways, they act as mentors for the prospects. Often mixed in with said prospects are the journeymen. Every league has journeyman-type players. They're a staple to any league.

You could say someone like Dominic Moore in the NHL is a journeyman-type player, because he's filled in role after role on many teams. In fact, as of this August as a free agent, Moore at age thirty-nine, has played on the same number of NHL teams as the fingers on your hands (including those much-debated thumbs). Ten.

At the AHL/ECHL level, let's pull a guy like Zach Tolkinen into the mix. A steady twenty-nine-year-old defenseman, Tolkinen has played nine AHL games to date, and they all came this past year. He's gotten a chance for the upcoming season with a con-tract for the Hartford Wolf Pack, though he is slated to begin the season back in the ECHL with Maine. However, he's played 311 ECHL games with five teams since beginning his professional career, even taking on leadership roles such as captain.

Even if going from club to club, it's not to say that these players aren't valued. They're like Swiss Army knives that are used for a variety of situations in a variety of instances, often making them the unsung heroes.

There are also the international journeymen, that have gone from league to league, played in a variety of leagues such as the NHL, the DEL (Deutsche Eishockey Liga), the AHL, the ECHL, or in some second-tiered European league that a casual hockey fan in North America would have no idea even existed. But, they're playing. And, there's no stopping them.

Mark Grainda, a writer for Sin Bin Hockey in a 2018 article said that:

Over the years, the Indy Fuel have had several very good players pack their bags and take their talents to Europe. For instance, former Fuel forward Alex Lavoie left Indy to play for BIK Karlskoga in the Swedish Second Division [HockeyAllsvenskan] and had 52 points in 51 games. Both Josh Shalla and Brady Ramsay left Indy for the EIHL [Elite Ice Hockey League, in the UK]; Shalla joining the Nottingham Panthers and Ramsay the Sheffield Steelers. The EIHL is a common league for ECHL and former AHL players to resort to. The majority of the time, play-ers just want to play. It becomes an issue of ice time.[4]

---

4   Grainda, Mark. 2018. "Why A Former ECHL Forward Headed Overseas." The Sin Bin.

Players that aren't looking for more than an elusive NHL call-up may make the change to Europe not for lack of experience in North American hockey, but rather because they value more ice time, more chances to play, and fulfill their love for the game.

It is quite obvious that in the hopeful call-up, the AHL and NHL have worked very closely together. It's a great prospect breeding ground for later picks, or talent that may not necessarily be ready for the NHL jump out of juniors, college, or other international professional leagues. There's no doubt that the AHL is the best professional developmental hockey league in the world—and if you disagree, I'd have to say that your "opinion," is wrong.

After the NHL and AHL, though, comes the ECHL, which takes on a very particular fascination. Being the AA developmental league, it gets a bad rap. I think that a lot of that bad rap is because, unlike the NHL, or even the AHL in most cases, the ECHL teams are subject to movement and aren't necessarily locked in one place; as you'll later read, it seems that teams are being suspended from the league, being added into the league, or dropping out of the league altogether on an almost yearly basis. Then comes the issue with affiliation contracts—which also seem to change on an almost yearly basis as well, for at least a couple of teams.

There's also an emphasis on entertainment value and afford-ability in watching games, but, isn't that what everyone wants?

While entertainment value is great, players are down there because they want to make a living playing the game they love. Prospects are down there because they were sent there to develop. Some players, who aren't even prospects, are just playing for a chance to go to the AHL, and potentially *become* someone's prospect. Others are seeing the "writing on the wall," and may move to a different league altogether, as mentioned previously.

Many see being sent down to the ECHL—especially if on an NHL contract—more of a demotion than a developmental phase. However, while it is technically a demotion going from a three-letter league to a four-letter league (the only notable three-letter league past the ECHL is the FHL [Federal Hockey League]—you don't particularly want to be sent all the way down there), players are able to get their bearings in profes-sional hockey, are given exponential playing time, and are given space to work on and fine tune their game.

Mike McKenna, a recently retired *journeyman* of the NHL, AHL, and ECHL, said in a 2010 article:

The ECHL is comprised primarily of players who have been overlooked by NHL teams for whatever reason. Many players thrive in this league yet – due to size, perceived skill level, or age (among other things) – have a difficult time getting a legitimate shot in the AHL (and subsequently NHL). However, this doesn't mean they are poor hockey players. If you take a quick glance at skills competition results from the ECHL, you'll find that some players are just as talented on an individual basis as those in the AHL and NHL. Guys can crank the puck over 100mph. They can skate a lap in under 14 seconds. [5]

So, if players are down there, for whatever reason, what's the big difference? Why hasn't the rate at which players progress from the ECHL to NHL gone up considerably?

The simple answer is that they're not fast enough. Not in a physical sense, but in hockey sense. Every player inherently works hard to get to the next level, but only the players who think the fastest while on the ice, and possess the greatest in-game intelligence and speed of mind are able to get to the AHL, and ultimately the NHL.

Shane Harper, former NHL, AHL, and ECHL player, said that the ECHL, where he started his professional career, gave him a rude awakening. Playing professionally allowed him to "get a little bit faster because you don't quite have as much time with the puck," and, as a result, process the game faster as well.

---

5   McKenna, Mike. 2010. "How Do The NHL, AHL And ECHL Differ - A Goalie's Perspective." InGoal Magazine.

As some NHL teams are more frequently utilizing ECHL teams in their prospect development, it comes with a certain level of trust.

For the first interview I had scheduled before sitting down and truly writing this book, I contacted David Farrar, the general manager of the Pennsylvania-based Reading Royals. The Royals are in an interesting situation based on the proximity of their affiliates. They're affiliated with the Lehigh Valley Phantoms who are less than an hour's drive away. The Phantoms, and thus the Royals, are affiliated with the Philadelphia Flyers, who are just about an hour away. There are three affiliations within the same system, all within an hour of each other.

When asked about expectations set forth by the Royals' parent clubs, the Lehigh Valley Phantoms and subsequently the Philadelphia Flyers, Farrar made mention of an element of trust. "The Flyers' management has complete trust in our coaching staff," Farrar said. "They trust us in developing their prospects."

The Flyers lacked depth this past year, and with the revolving door of goaltenders at the NHL level, the Royals' hadn't seen too much sent their way. For this upcoming year, the Royals expect some fresh faces, though, as the Flyers made seven picks during the 2019 NHL Entry Draft.

It was trust from the Flyers, down to the Phantoms, and eventually leading to the Royals, that players would be properly developed in any given circumstance. The Royals, though they hadn't received any notable prospects during the 2018–19 season, were being trusted by the parent clubs that whoever they did receive, even if in the next year, would thrive in an ECHL environment to be shaped into higher quality players at higher levels.

Reading, as an ECHL franchise, has played a part in the development of forty NHL players to date, which is over 6 percent of all ECHL players to ever hit the NHL. With twenty-six current teams and many players developed through teams now defunct, this is a very impressive feat.

Trust. Trust is key.

So many foundational principles are built on trust. Players will be taken care of, will be given the amenities they need to succeed, will be given opportunities, and will ultimately develop based off of trust that runs through the veins of an organization.

One of the ECHL's newest franchises, the Maine Mariners, had been trusted by the New York Rangers organization and the AHL's Hartford Wolf Pack to develop players. Four NHL-contracted players with the Rangers made their way through Maine this past season—including; Brandon Halverson, Chris Nell, Sean Day, and Ty Ronning. Out of the fifty-eight total players for the Mariners this season, twenty-two were at some point during the season called up to the AHL level, signaling strong development of many of the players. All four of the previous players mentioned were called up to the AHL throughout the season. Additionally, Halverson and Day finished the season in the AHL.

As of free agency this year, the Rangers chose not to qualify offers to Halverson or Nell, which signaled the end of their time with the Rangers organization, at least for the time being. Ronning and Day are on their entry-level contracts, and are slated to start the season with the Mariners and Wolf Pack, respectively.

The thing about prospect development is this: Sometimes, it works out really well. Other times, it doesn't. And there's a huge "in-between," in which many players float in the middle of being good, or not good enough. Only time will tell how these players will turn out, but it's evident when prospect development is done right by an organization.

CHAPTER 3

A BRIEF HISTORY OF THE EAST COAST HOCKEY LEAGUE

———

Before getting into the rest of the book, a history lesson is needed about the ECHL, including its origins and progression toward an elite professional hockey league.

First and foremost, the ECHL is the premier AA developmental professional hockey league in North America.

The East Coast Hockey League, or "E" as some have called it, began in 1988 with founder Henry Brabham, with just five teams combining from the Atlantic Coast Hockey League and All-American Hockey League. The teams were the Erie

Panthers, Johnstown Chiefs, Knoxville Cherokees, Carolina Thunderbirds, and Virginia Lancers. The first commissioner of the league was Patrick J. Kelly.[6]

Some thirty-one years later, in 2019, the Brabham Cup, honoring Henry Brabham, is given to the team with the most points in the league at the end of the regular season, and the Kelly Cup, honoring Patrick J. Kelly, as the league's championship trophy. [7]

In the 1989–90 season, the Greensboro Monarchs, Hampton Roads Admirals and Nashville Knights were added to the league, making the ECHL an eight-team league. A historic milestone is hit, as Scott Gordon becomes first player to play in the National Hockey League after playing in the ECHL, taking the ice for the now-defunct Quebec Nordiques on January 30, 1990.[8]

In 1990–91, the Cincinnati Cyclones, Louisville IceHawks, and Richmond Renegades were added to bring the league to eleven teams.[9]

---

6   "ECHL History." 2019. Echl.Com.
7   Ibid.
8   Ibid.
9   Ibid.

In 1991–92, the Columbus Chill, Dayton Bombers, Raleigh IceCaps, and Toledo Storm were all added to the league to bring the total to fifteen teams.[10]

In 1993–94, the Charlotte Checkers, Huntington Blizzard, Roanoke Express, and South Carolina Stingrays were added, making the ECHL a nineteen-team league.[11]

1994–95 was a very successful year for the league. Goaltenders Manon Rheaume and Erin Whitten—the first two female hockey players to play men's professional hockey, recorded their first two professional wins. Additionally, former Cincinnati defenseman Kevin Dean became the first ECHL player to have his name engraved on the Stanley Cup as a member of the New Jersey Devils.[12]

1995–96 was another historic year for the ECHL. The Greensboro Monarchs return their ECHL membership and join the American Hockey League. The Louisiana IceGators, Louisville RiverFrogs, and Mobile Mysticks are added, making the ECHL a twenty-one-team league. The league's first website was also launched. The league office gets relocated from Charlotte, North Carolina, to Princeton, New Jersey. The league launches ECHL Properties, the licensing and marketing arm

---

10   Ibid.
11   Ibid.
12   Ibid.

of the ECHL. The league unveils a new logo designed by NHL Enterprises, Inc. and announces a new national licensing program with the NHL. The league then executes its first Collective Bargaining Agreement with the Professional Hockey Players' Association, better known as the PHPA.[13]

In 1996–97, the Mississippi Sea Wolves and Peoria Rivermen are added, making the ECHL a twenty-three-team league. The South Carolina Stingrays become the first team in league history to win the regular season championship and postseason championship in the same season. The Patrick J. Kelly Cup replaces the Jack Riley Cup as trophy awarded to postseason champion. Patrick J. Kelly is named Commissioner Emeritus. [14]

In 1997–98, the Chesapeake Icebreakers and New Orleans Brass are added, making the ECHL a twenty-five-team league. The NHL then awards former Richmond goaltender, Jamie McLennan of the St. Louis Blues, the Bill Masterton Memorial Trophy. [15]McLennan overcame a life-threatening bacterial meningitis diagnosis after the 1995–96 season, missed most of the 1996–97 season, and returned in 1997–98 to take over the Blues' net as Grant Fuhr went out with an injury. [16]

---

13   Ibid.
14   Ibid.
15   Ibid.
16   Elliott, Helene. 1998. "Goaltender Mclennan's Biggest Save Was His Life." Los Angeles Times.

1998–99 sees the Florida Everblades and Greenville Grrrowl added, making the ECHL a twenty-seven-team league. [17]

1999–00 saw Columbus and Miami granted voluntary suspension. Voluntary suspension is when a team typically requests to cease hockey operations for the next season, often because of insecurity financially, problems with the arena in which they play, or other issues that directly or indirectly prevent the team from being able to fulfill operations necessary to play in the season. The Arkansas RiverBlades, Greensboro Generals, and Trenton Titans are added, making the ECHL a twenty-eight-team league. Former Raleigh left wing Krzysztof Oliwa becomes the second former ECHL player to have his name engraved on the Stanley Cup as a member of the New Jersey Devils. The NHL awards former Hampton Roads goaltender Olaf Kolzig the Vezina Trophy.[18]

In 2000–01, Hampton Roads, Huntington, and Jacksonville are granted voluntary suspension, making the ECHL a twenty-five-team league. Former Chesapeake and Wheeling goaltender David Aebischer and Richmond defenseman Nolan Pratt become the third and fourth former ECHL players to have their names engraved on the Stanley Cup as members of

---

17 "ECHL History." 2019. Echl.Com.
18 Ibid.

the Colorado Avalanche. This is the first time multiple ECHL players have been on Stanley Cup champion.[19]

In 2001–02, it's the year of the transferring teams. The Columbia Inferno are added, making the ECHL a twenty-nine-team league.[20]

In 2002–03, Mobile and New Orleans are granted voluntary suspensions, making the ECHL a twenty-seven-team league. Brian McKenna is named the President/Chief Executive Officer (CEO). The league name was officially changed from the East Coast Hockey League to the ECHL on May 19, 2003.[21]

In 2003–04, Arkansas and Jacksonville returned their ECHL memberships. The ECHL expands into the western United States with the addition of the expansion members the Alaska Aces, Bakersfield Condors, Fresno Falcons, Idaho Steelheads, Las Vegas Wranglers, Long Beach Ice Dogs, and San Diego Gulls from the now defunct West Coast Hockey League, making the ECHL a thirty-one-team league.[22]

In 2004–05, Baton Rouge is transferred to Victoria and is renamed the Victoria Salmon Kings becoming the ECHL's

---

19   Ibid.
20   Ibid.
21   Ibid.
22   Ibid.

first club based in Canada. Cincinnati and Columbus are granted voluntary suspension and memberships in Greensboro and Roanoke are terminated, while Richmond voluntarily returns its membership, making the ECHL a twenty-eight-team league.[23]

In 2005–06, Pee Dee is granted voluntary suspension, the Louisiana membership is terminated, and Peoria joins the AHL. Mississippi is forced to cancel their season because of Hurricane Katrina and Texas is forced to cancel their season because of Hurricane Rita, making the ECHL a twenty-five-team league.[24]

Over the next six years, teams started to diminish. By the 2011–12 season, only twenty teams were active, by way of two expansion teams while one of the more historic teams—the Victoria Salmon Kings, dropped out of the equation. The ECHL was represented on the Stanley Cup for the 12th year in a row and Jonathan Quick becomes the second consecutive ECHL alum to win the Conn Smythe Trophy as Most Valuable Player of the Stanley Cup Playoffs, following Tim Thomas of the Boston Bruins in the 2010–11 season. [25]

By 2014–15—only three years after being only twenty teams— the ECHL again rose back up to twenty-eight teams, as the

---

23 Ibid.
24 Ibid.
25 Ibid.

ECHL accepted expansion members in Allen, Brampton, Indy, Missouri, Quad City, Rapid City, Tulsa and Wichita while Las Vegas is granted a voluntary suspension.[26]

In the 2016–17 season, the ECHL saw its 600th alumnus play in an NHL game—Florida Panthers forward, Shane Harper.[27]

The 2017–18 season saw the one hundred millionth fan turn out for an ECHL game, in a season in which the thirtieth anniversary of the ECHL was celebrated. After the season, league commissioner Brian McKenna would step down.[28]

For the 2018–19 season, the league would lower to twenty-seven teams, with Ryan Crelin taking over as league commissioner. The league would welcome several expansion teams—with the Newfoundland Growlers, one of said teams, ultimately winning the Kelly Cup. On the down side, the Manchester Monarchs ceased operations by the end of the season, bringing the amount of teams to twenty-six for the 2019–20 season.[29]

By the end of the 2018-19 season, 662 players in total have seen NHL action, and developed at the ECHL level at some point in their careers.

---

26 Ibid.
27 Ibid.
28 Ibid.
29 Ibid.

For a more complete timeline, please use the following link address to see the timeline in its entirety:

www.echl.com/en/pages/echl-history

PART 2

LET'S MEET SOME PLAYERS

I was able to talk to and interview several players whose journeys have all involved the ECHL. Three of the players have gone from the ECHL and worked their way to the NHL, including two who made their debut this past regular season. For these three players, they all played over sixty games in the ECHL, which I felt was necessary to mention. They were seasoned. One of the players made it to the AHL this year, earning an AHL contract.

While their stories are different and intriguing in their own ways, they exemplify what it means to develop as professional players, progressing through one stage and onto the next. In the face of adversity, they persevere. When they've been given a chance, they've made the most of it.

Additionally, I wrote a story on a rare sort of player, someone that without a doubt in my mind is the best ECHL player I had seen play live in the 2018–19 ECHL season.

For each player, I've added some basic information, as well as some statistics, to help follow along with each individual story; these statistics do not take into account *playoff* statistics and are strictly *regular season,* to properly clarify. All statistics are through the 2018–19 season.

CHAPTER 4

SHANE HARPER

Date of Birth: February 1, 1989

Birthplace: Valencia, California, USA

Position: Right Wing

Statistics to Note:

Year	Team	League	Games Played	Goals	Assists	Total Points	Penalty Minutes	Plus/ Minus
2009–2010	Everett Silvertips	WHL	72	42	38	80	38	36
	Adirondack Phantoms	AHL	5	1	0	1	2	-1
2010–2011	Adirondack Phantoms	AHL	20	1	2	3	4	-9
	Greenville Swamp Rabbits	ECHL	48	22	23	45	20	18
2011–2012	Adirondack Phantoms	AHL	70	13	14	27	43	-9
2012–2013	Adirondack Phantoms	AHL	48	5	5	10	35	-17
	Trenton Titans	ECHL	15	14	13	27	2	3
2013–2014	Chicago Wolves	AHL	63	13	20	33	8	19
2014–2015	Chicago Wolves	AHL	75	32	18	50	14	-4
2015–2016	Portland Pirates	AHL	59	12	25	37	18	-6
2016–2017	Florida Panthers	NHL	14	2	1	3	18	-1
	Springfield Thunderbirds	AHL	39	7	12	19	6	-4
	Albany Devils	AHL	19	1	2	3	2	-5
2017–2018	Lada Togliatti	KHL	36	4	7	11	13	-15
2018–2019	Örebro HK	SHL	52	9	19	28	14	-6

30

In any professional sports league, you just never know when the game you play in a city you love may be your last.

The Portland Pirates of the AHL were sold out from underneath everyone in the Pirates' organization, and the City of Portland in the unfortunate Spring of 2016. Take Mike McKenna, the ultimate journeyman goaltender, who made these comments on an Instagram post on June 28, 2016:

---

30 "Elite Prospects - Shane Harper." Elite Prospects, 2019.

Sometimes I feel like a city killer...Lowell, MA bit the dust after the season I played there, along with Peoria, IL. Now you can add Portland. Omaha (AHL) is toast, Norfolk (AHL) is now ECHL. And my ECHL Alma Mater, the Las Vegas Wranglers, have been gone for a few years. What does this really all mean? That minor league hockey is an ever changing landscape, and nothing is forever. Once you think you've seen it all, something happens to remind you that life is full of surprises. Here's to the future.[31]

A great future McKenna had—though he still managed to make many more unexpected pit stops along the way. Mike, if you're reading this, you're always welcome back to Portland, for even more lobster.

McKenna wasn't the only one whose scenery took an unexpected change from the great state of Maine. In fact, every other player on that roster suddenly had to pack up their bags and move.

A close family friend of mine, Brad Perry, recalled that then-Pirates player Shane Harper walked into his workplace the day the team was announced to be moving. Brad and his girlfriend, Jacki, were (and to be fair, still are) big fans of Shane. Brad had asked Shane earlier in the season if there was

---

31   McKenna, Mike. 'PHPA Annual Meeting.' Instagram. June 28, 2016.

any way he could get a signed stick for Jacki, since he was one of her favorite minor league players. Shane happily obliged.

Brad said, "So the day they announced the team was moving everybody at work was talking about it. Then with five minutes before close, there were three of us working. We saw headlights pull into the parking lot." Rather comedically, he continued, "We're like 'ahh $#!&.' Hopefully this is quick so we can get out of here." He wasn't looking when the person came in, but one of his coworkers goes, "Huh. He's got a stick. Wonder what he needs?"

It was Shane Harper, with the stick he had promised several weeks earlier.

Harper was undoubtedly a fan favorite in Portland. In March, he was even named the team's winner of the IOA/American Specialty AHL Man of the Year award for his outstanding contributions to the Greater Portland community during the 2015–16 season.[32]

With the relocation of the Portland Pirates to Springfield, the home of the AHL's headquarters, another offseason began for the winger, who had just finished his seventh professional season, bouncing between two leagues and five teams.

---

32 "Man Of The Year Team Award Winners Named". 2016. Theahl.Com.

Yet, just several months later, he found himself on the Florida Panthers roster, in the lineup, on the opening night of the 2016–17 NHL season. His debut made him the 600th ECHL player to hit the NHL. Nine days later, on October 22, Harper would score two goals—the first two goals of his NHL career.

We have to rewind a little bit though, to understand how he got to that moment. In fact, let's rewind all the way to March 4, 2010. Harper was still in Canada's junior ranks, playing for the Everett Silvertips, and was noticed and signed by the Philadelphia Flyers to a future contract that would start at the beginning of the 2010–11 season. Harper was undrafted, and made his way onto the Flyers' AHL affiliate, the Adirondack Phantoms.

He would split time between the Phantoms and the Flyers' ECHL affiliate, the Greenville Road Warriors.

Harper, in his initial reaction to being sent down to the ECHL, said, "I was 21 years old, I wasn't familiar with the ECHL at all, so I wasn't happy and I just thought oh, 'What is this? What does this mean?' I really had no idea until I got there, and I was really surprised at the caliber of hockey."

While his numbers weren't all too well at the AHL level, he was producing at nearly a point-per-game basis at the ECHL level, with forty-five points in forty-eight games, and tacking on ten points in eleven games of the ECHL postseason. It wasn't the league he had expected to be in, but it was a great first professional season. He was starting to get *noticed*. He was starting to perform at a very high level, very quickly, turning the heads in other leagues and organizations.

"Obviously the NHL is so competitive which feeds down to the AHL, which is so competitive, and there's so many guys that could be in the AHL, but there's not enough room, so ... obviously where do they go? They go into the ECHL, but when you're young you probably don't realize that, and I didn't," said Harper.

This is a true quote on many levels. Which, as I'll talk about later, is why it's so important that the ECHL expands so that there are teams affiliated with every NHL team. Players don't have enough outlets to go to if they can't compete at the AHL level, and either can't be sent down, or move on to another league. Continuing on about Harper, though. The level of production that he sustained gave him another shot at cracking the AHL lineup. He didn't disappoint anyone.

In turn, he saw himself on the Adirondack Phantoms' roster in 2011–12, for the entire season. His work ethic and drive to compete paid off in January of 2012, when he scored the overtime winner against the Hershey Bears in the AHL's third outdoor game, and heads began to turn, including

Chris Pryor, former Flyers Director of Hockey Operations, who said, "I think down the road, because he has a good attitude, good work ethic and competitiveness, he's going to give himself a chance."[33]

That chance didn't come from the Flyers, though. Harper would, like many players at some point in their career, have a down year with the Phantoms in 2012–13, only notching seven points in forty-one games before being sent down for the second time that year to the new ECHL affiliate of the Flyers, the Trenton Thunder.

"I remember being told, in the office, and I was disappointed, but also, once you are around it for a couple of years, you can kinda guess what's gonna happen. So, I think I knew it was a possibility, maybe at that time I wasn't playing much, maybe I was in and out of the line-up." It's one of those things that may happen. Sometimes, the writing is on the wall. And then, it happens. It's an unexpected jolt.

Even though he was sent down, Harper remained positive, and with a good attitude toward the shift to a lower level yet again. "I've always had a good attitude. I think that's important for players in the future to learn from ... You know, you're frustrated, you don't ever want to be sent down, but

---

33   Staff Writer. "Future Watch: Shane Harper". 2012. NHL.Com.

you kinda have to look at it as an opportunity and almost let the guys know that, that it is the team that you wanna be on, that you can be there and you should be there." Positivity is key. "I went into it with a good attitude. I like to have fun. I like to smile." Maintaining that positivity would allow him room to flourish, being given more playing time and more opportunities on a nightly basis.

His time in the ECHL would come to an end after finishing his season with a remarkable goal-per-game pace, with twelve goals in twelve games, and adding eleven assists, for twenty-three points. This would be the last time Harper would see ice at the ECHL level. The change in scenery had seemingly revitalized his confidence, as he was going from a healthy scratch here and there, to scoring goals again, getting playing time night after night.

Regarding his time and effort put into the ECHL level, he said, "it was the best thing that could've happened for me because I think I was a little undeveloped as a player to be ready for a full NHL season. I think the skills were there, but, jumping up into pro hockey from major junior, it's a big jump… I got to play a lot after I kind of figured it out, and I got to continue my skills and develop my skills as a player, maybe get a little bit faster, because you don't quite have as much time with the puck," compared to the junior level. You have to think faster. You can't be indecisive.

Harper continued to grind and work for his dream. He wasn't letting anything phase him, or waver his determination.

Over the next three seasons, he would play 197 regular season AHL contests, recording a very respectable 120 points. He split time between the Chicago Wolves, and the Portland Pirates. This brings us back to the beginning of the story— you know—how I said that the Pirates were sold out from underneath everyone back in 2016. At this point, Shane has been signed in the Florida Panthers organization for a little over a year. And, shortly after the end of the Pirates' season, he's re-signed with the Panthers, another two-way contract, but another chance and another step closer to "the dream."[34]

As the 2016–17 season rolled around, Shane found himself competing for not only another chance, but an NHL roster spot. As the September training camp passed, his hard work paid off when he was rewarded with a spot on the fourth line. He made his debut on October 13, 2016, on the opening night roster for the Panthers.

It took six years of professional hockey to make it into his first NHL game. On top of that, it took five seasons of Western Hockey League action. Eleven years of development across various leagues for his first chance at the NHL level.

---

34 Staff Writer. "Florida Panthers Re-Sign Forward Shane Harper". 2016. NHL.Com.

"No matter where you are, you just have to try to make the best of it, and it does make it that much sweeter for sure, getting that first NHL game after, you know," Harper said. He reflected on the journey, too, which was all but a smooth one. "All the ups and downs, the hard work you put in. It was a long road, but I think it makes it that much sweeter, and you can appreciate that much more."

Just nine days later, he scored the first two goals of his NHL career on the same night, and proceed to toss in a fighting major as well.

Harper would only see a handful more games of NHL action(for now), registering a total of two goals and one assist in fourteen games, before being sent back down to the AHL.

Following the AHL season, Harper relocated, and continued his journey of professional hockey, going to Russia for a season in the Kontinental Hockey League, and then traveling to Sweden in 2018–19, to play in the Swedish Hockey League, where he remains signed for the 2019–20 season with Örebro HK.

It's been quite the journey to this point. But, it seems as if he wouldn't change a thing. He joins a pretty small list of players, in the grand scheme of things. "I'm proud to be a player from the ECHL that played in an NHL game. I think that was a pretty cool thing."

When he's in the offseason, he resides in the Adirondack Thunder's area, and has been to a few ECHL-level games there. "The hockey's great. It's exciting, and I like to support those guys as well, so I'm obviously a big advocate for the ECHL."

That's the stuff I like to hear.

CHAPTER 5

CONNOR LACOUVEE

Date of Birth: May 24, 1994

Birthplace: Qualicum Beach, British Columbia, Canada

Position: Goaltender

Statistics to Note:

Year	Team	League	Games Played	GAA	SV%
2018–2019	Maine Mariners	ECHL	20	3.22	0.913
	Utica Comets	AHL	3	2.87	0.877
	Laval Rocket	AHL	14	2.49	0.913

35

While the ECHL is a development league, sometimes teams have to take a shot in the dark. It's a somewhat educated shot in the dark. If it weren't educated, it wouldn't be pro hockey. It would be "Be a GM" mode, in NHL 20. Or, men's league, in which you take the goaltender that's readily available if yours is still at the bar. But, you have to realize that there are many players that have had one to two game stints at the ECHL level only to be forgotten about. It's not that these players are bad players, by any means. Some can't crack the lineup, others don't fill the mold that had initially been needed and wanted. Some are just there to sub in for an injury, only to be released. Many players have skill and talent, but can't think in the moment fast enough to compete at a higher level. Or, in some unfortunate cases, never crack the pros at all.

With this being said, there are some players able to make a name for themselves against all odds, and here's one of them, who I've had the pleasure of watching develop from a third string

---

35   "Elite Prospects - Connor LaCouvee." Elite Prospects, 2019.

relatively unknown ECHL backup goaltender to a time-sharing AHL goaltender. A goaltender, who just recently signed an AHL contract with the Laval Rocket, and played in the Montréal Canadiens' June 2019 prospect developmental camp.

Again, let's rewind a little though. Let's rewind all the way back to March 2019.

"Wild Blueberries" night, at the ECHL's Maine Mariners home arena, the Cross Insurance Arena. March 9, 2019, to be exact. It was also voted the ECHL's "Theme Night of the Year" in June.

It was a night dedicated to the "what-if" for the fan vote for the team name, that had happened what seems like ages ago. While the Mariners were selected as the team's name, "Wild Blueberries" came in second. Add it to the list of ridiculous minor professional sports team names. The Swamp Rabbits, the Solar Bears, and heck, let's mix the Rumble Ponies and Yard Goats in just for good measure.

The players were announced as the Wild Blueberries, for this one special night, wearing light blue and comical jerseys and socks, with a sort of comic-sans font for the nameplate.

Fans entering the arena were given wild blueberry-themed cups (mine still remains in pristine condition, it is for sale), and upon exiting were given complimentary Oakhurst Dairy wild blueberry flavored milk, which was nothing short of absolutely delicious.

Merchandise from shirts to baseball caps with the Wild Blueberries logos were being tossed out left and right, and season ticketholders were trying to rationalize how the season would have gone had this actually been the team's name.

As the game began, it was an electric atmosphere. It became a goaltending duel immediately, with each goalie going practically save-for-save with each other. At one point, I remember yelling, "KEEP IT UP COUVEE!!" The people to my left asked if I knew the guy. I said a little, that he was a cool guy, and I had met him a few times. It was a classically sarcastic, "you could say I'm a pretty big deal," moment.

Despite the great effort by both goaltenders, in the game of hockey, one must always lose.

Connor LaCouvee let in a shot through a screen in overtime, above his leg pad and below his glove, and the Wild Blueberries lost their only game ever. Not a great winning percentage, there.

"What did you think about Wild Blueberries Night at the Mariners?" I asked.

"That was pretty cool. I wish we won though."

"Yeah? That would have been nice."

"Dude we lost that game, right?"

"Yeah, you gave up a goal in overtime. Yup."

A saddened goaltender, he responded, "I wish you didn't remind me of this."

My bad, buddy. My bad. At least the blueberry milk was good.

After the game, the jerseys would be auctioned off to some lucky fans, and you bet I stayed around to bid. Not to bid on LaCouvee, though. I had my eyes on the jersey of the Alex Burrows-like character on the Mariners, Greg Chase. Or perhaps, the smallest guy on our team, Taylor Cammarata. He was 5'7, 161. I'm 6'5, 220. It would have been a funny jersey to try and fit into. Maybe, just maybe, I'd try and snag one of the weirdest jerseys I've ever seen—that of Chris Ordoobadi's.

The nameplate didn't come in time for the game, so equipment manager Mark "Ripper" Riepe had to individually piece together letters from other jerseys, and use navy sharpie. In an absolute worst-case scenario event, Ripper ran out of extra Os and had to stitch on a o. Desperate measure, for sure.

The last jersey auction for the team had been the Maine Mariners' throwback jerseys, and goaltender Brandon Halverson's jersey went for over $1k. As arena emcee Lizzie Muse would say, "That's a whole lot of dough!" Especially for a college student.

I expected LaCouvee to go for around the same, being the starting goaltender with a battered jersey.

The auction went by faster than I had initially expected, and all of a sudden, there were just a few jerseys left. I bid on our backup-goaltender Hannu Toivonen's jersey (yes, that's Hannu Toivonen, the former Boston Bruins' first round pick), knowing full well that LaCouvee was coming up. I lost the Toivonen jersey to my friend, who was brave enough to outbid me.

We're still friends, if you were wondering.

LaCouvee came next, and you bet I expected the worst, but came out with guns blazing.

$250!

$300.

$350!

$400.

$425.

$450!

$475.

$500!

$525.

$550!

Going once... Going twice... SOLD!

I was suddenly the confused, yet proud owner of a one of a kind Wild Blueberries jersey, drenched in sweat (the jersey, not me), and battered with puck marks. I got up to pay for my item and insisted that it went for $525, but I was wrong. $25 wasn't going to kill me, either, though. Sorry for arguing on the number, Parker.

LaCouvee waited for me as I took my grand old time getting to him, and we talked for a bit like two old tenders (twenty-two and twenty-four years old, so definitely old), and I had him sign the fight strap, like any good jersey collector knows. He's a pro goalie, I was an ACHA DII goalie. I'd say we're pretty close in skill.

* * *

Before the rosters had been announced in training camp in Maine this past season, LaCouvee was the last player that coach Riley Armstrong waited to hear from on signing with the brand-new team. Though there seemed to be some deliberation on whether LaCouvee was going to sign on in the NBC Sports mini-documentary series, *Puckland*, it seemed to me in talking to him, that he had his eyes locked on Maine the entire time.

"I was really excited to sign in Maine. I had heard Portland was a really beautiful place." It is, he's not wrong. But also, he was "really excited for the team they were putting together," and "had heard a lot of great things about Riley Armstrong as well, about how he coaches, how he is as a person. I just heard a lot of positives from him, and just how he described the team as well and described Portland."

Armstrong was equally as excited for the young goaltender to come to Maine. "When I was with the Penguins, I went to development camp with them and Mike Hastings, who was Connor's coach at Mankato. He was at development camp as a guest coach and I got to build a little bit of a relationship with Mike and come summertime last year Mike called me and said, 'hey, I think I got a really good goalie for ya.' "

And his name was Connor.

"So I was able to give Connor a call and see if he wanted to come."

Connor LaCouvee was third on the new Maine Mariners' depth chart at the start of the season back in October 2018. Chris Nell and Brandon Halverson, both New York Rangers signed goaltending prospects at the time, were elected as the one-two punch for the beginning of what would be a rollercoaster season. In the *Puckland* documentary mentioned earlier, Mariners' head coach, Riley Armstrong, mentioned that he believed LaCouvee had a chance to be an elite goaltender at the ECHL level, maybe even the AHL level.

Halverson and Nell played out the first three games of the season to a surprising and underwhelming 0-and-3 record, a far cry from what those in attendance, management, coaches, and players had hoped for. The goalie behind those two was fresh out of the NCAA's first division, and soon found himself between the pipes for game 4, in his first ever professional start.

Truly, being a season ticketholder, it seemed like Armstrong was just praying that maybe this unheralded goaltender could get something going, as an 0-and-4 start is immeasurably worse than 0-and-3, especially when it's the "postgame skate with the team," immediately following the game. Depressed players and fans alike isn't the best combination for that kind of event.

LaCouvee stopped thirty-two out of thirty-four shots as the Maine Mariners picked up the first win of their "new" existence. It was his first professional win. Almost in a Jordan Binnington-esque response, when asked about that experience, he said, "That was pretty cool. It was pretty awesome." A man of few words.

I prompted for a little more, and he gave a little more. "It was really fun. I mean, just nice to see the guys excited and happy. It was just nice knowing some of the hard work and commitment had paid off."

He, in one Sunday afternoon as the third-string goalie, changed his name for the future. People took notice.

LaCouvee was soon loaned to Utica of the AHL, posting numbers that were less than spectacular. "I don't think I really had the best mindset when I was in Utica. They told me I was just going to be back and out and I'm not really playing any games. So I guess it was my first time with the AHL experience. I guess I was just kind of there to learn and take it in, but I really didn't."

A 2.87 Goals Against Average (GAA) and .877 Save Percentage (SV%) may have suggested that he wasn't quite ready for the AHL, and the mind-set in place certainly didn't help.[36] The Vancouver Canucks' top goaltending prospect Thatcher Demko was due back soon for the Comets, to resume his workload and push LaCouvee back to the ECHL.

By the end of December, LaCouvee was back up to the AHL, but this time for the Laval Rocket. At the end of six games, LaCouvee had earned an AHL contract for Laval for the rest of the season, posting a 1.98 GAA and .927 SV%, both largely improved numbers from his short time in Utica.[37] When he got his first AHL win in his first game with Laval, it was a sigh of relief.

"A win is a win but it was just getting my first one especially coming out of the hardship I went through in Utica and not getting to start and then when I got a start I didn't play as well as I wanted. So it was nice to play my first game and again just nice to see that hard work paying off." The AHL, of course, is also one league above where he'd gotten his first professional win, several months earlier. I asked him what he really thought of that first AHL win and his true colors shone through.

---

36 Ibid.
37 Ibid.

"I mean, three letters. Three letter league. It was pretty hot, you know?"

Four letters in college to a four-letter pro league, and now a three-letter league? *Pretty hot stuff* right there.

In early February of 2019, after signing his contract for Laval, he was sent back down to Maine, and gradually took over the starting role as Halverson was called up to the Hartford Wolf Pack. In twenty games this past year in the ECHL, 'Couvee posted a 3.22 GAA and a .913 SV%. While that 3.22 is at first glance an incredibly ugly number to look at, the save percentage is quite remarkable, insisting that the goaltender did face a high quantity of shots (and many quality shots, at that) on a nightly basis.

He's gone from someone who was a third-string backup on a struggling ECHL team, to a relied upon starting goaltender in minor league professional hockey, making a name for himself, and getting yet another call-up to Laval in early March. But, he's still got a long way to go, and he knows it. The NHL is the dream.

"I mean there's quite a few goalies that have played in the coast and now play in the NHL. There's six goalies in a system, right? You could have an NHL goalie that's a trend starter, that's been there for a couple of years so you're not going to be jumping in taking that spot." At least, not immediately.

"And sometimes they have a pretty solid older backup that's been doing that position so you might not be able to ever jump in and take that spot right away," LaCouvee said.

As an undrafted free agent, he knew he'd have to pay his dues at lower levels. "It's just all part of the process." Trust the process, as they say.

On June 18, 2019, the Laval Rocket announced that they had signed the netminder to a one-year, two-way deal, allowing him to split between the AHL and ECHL. [38]

The following week, he was off to the Montréal Canadiens' prospect development camp. With the recent signing of Keith Kinkaid by Montréal to backup arguably the best goaltender in the world, Carey Price, Laval is currently stuffed to the brim with goaltending talent. Charlie Lindgren, Cayden Primeau, Michael McNiven, and Connor LaCouvee will be battling the entire season for AHL action, most likely resulting in one or two of these goalies being sent back down to the ECHL level for further seasoning, or even traded away altogether. For now, LaCouvee is one of the odd men out, starting the season with Maine. Michael McNiven is also starting the season in Adirondack.

---

38   MacMillan, Ken. 2019. "Montreal Canadiens Re-Sign Connor Lacouvee". A Winning Habit.

However, this time, it's quite clear that he's not going to be a third string backup.

We will have to wait and see how it all plays out.

CHAPTER 6

JACOB MACDONALD

Date of Birth: February 26, 1993

Birthplace: Portland, Oregon, USA

Position: Defense

Statistics to Note:

Year	Team	League	Games Played	Goals	Assists	Total Points	Penalty Minutes	Plus/ Minus
2011–2012	Cornell University	NCAA	8	0	1	1	2	3
2012–2013	Cornell University	NCAA	33	0	3	3	39	-1
2013–2014	Cornell University	NCAA	32	2	6	8	4	6
2014–2015	Cornell University	NCAA	31	2	7	9	8	-7
2015–2016	Elmira Jackals	ECHL	8	1	2	3	2	-2
	Elmira Jackals	ECHL	72	17	20	37	34	11
	Springfield Falcons	AHL	1	0	0	0	0	-1
2016–2017	Toledo Walleye	ECHL	30	7	19	26	24	12
	Albany Devils	AHL	34	8	16	24	9	-4
2017–2018	Binghamton Devils	AHL	75	20	35	55	35	-26
2018–2019	Florida Panthers	NHL	2	1	0	1	0	1
	Springfield Thunderbirds	AHL	72	14	29	43	27	-2

39

As a kid growing up watching and playing hockey, you always dream about being drafted by your favorite team, scoring your first goal, and winning the Stanley Cup—often on an overtime goal by yourself on an amazing individual effort.

Or, maybe, that was just me. But, I like to think that it wasn't.

For the vast majority of all hockey players, any combination of any of those things happening, even standalone, is extremely rare.

---

39 "Elite Prospects - Jacob MacDonald." Elite Prospects, 2019.

To get one of those things is a blessing.

Jacob MacDonald went undrafted. 0-for-1 on the list for him.

Not only did he go undrafted, but he also finished his college hockey career on a Division I Cornell University hockey club that only managed to score fifty-seven goals in thirty-one games, the lowest goal total in their history. The Cornell Big Red had eleven wins, six ties, and fourteen losses in the 2014–15 season. Which, actually, isn't that bad considering the lack of goal scoring. The team survived on great goaltending and defensive play.[40] Without those two factors, it could have been a much worse season. In fact, the starting goaltender for Cornell, Mitch Gillam, is currently a goaltender for the Wichita Thunder. Some of MacDonald's fellow defensemen were Patrick McCarron, who played on the Florida Everblades this past year, and Joakim Ryan, who just signed with the Los Angeles Kings and has over one hundred NHL games under his belt. The roster contained plenty of players that have played AHL, ECHL, or international professional hockey.

Straight out of college, MacDonald did get some interest, but from Southern Professional Hockey League (SPHL) teams. "One thing I did know is that I wanted to play in the East

---

40 "Elite Prospects - 2014-15 Cornell University" Elite Prospects, 2019.

Coast Hockey League." His chance came with Jamie Russell, the head coach of the Elmira Jackals, who helped him through the transition.

If you were looking at strictly statistics on paper, you wouldn't have expected much from the senior defenseman, Jacob MacDonald, finishing his year at Cornell. However, what you see on a stat line doesn't always tell the full story. MacDonald had four goals and seventeen assists in 104 career NCAA games, which doesn't exactly scream offensive potential. However, looking at his numbers in juniors, he put up respectable offensive totals.

MacDonald described to me, in the comparison of ECHL hockey to NCAA hockey, "it's a little bit more of an open back and forth style of hockey," and that "it's just significantly more offensive." There isn't as much offensive freedom in the NCAA, or at least, for Cornell.

"I have to give a lot of credit to Jamie Russell, who gave me every opportunity. I wasn't really on the power play at Cornell for any of my four years. That's become the staple of my game since day one in pro hockey."

The first eight games he played after joining Elmira, the offensive side started to shine through a little bit more. He had one goal and two assists.

In his first full year of professional hockey with Elmira in 2015–16, he registered seventeen goals and twenty assists. Among defensemen, he tied for first in goals, tenth in points, and made the All-Rookie Team. He also earned a quick one-game loan to the AHL's Springfield Falcons. He was dealt to the Toledo Walleye at the end of the season.

In Toledo, his numbers were seven goals and nineteen assists in just thirty games, before being loaded to the AHL's Albany Devils. He was named as a starter for the 2017 ECHL All-Star Game, but was unable to play because of the loan. Toledo would be his last stop in the ECHL, accumulating a total of twenty-five goals and forty-one assists in 110 total contests. Finishing the season in Albany, he'd post similar numbers to his ECHL numbers. Eight goals and sixteen assists in thirty-four games.

As the Albany Devils became the Binghamton Devils in 2017–18, the ECHL All-Rookie Team defensive standout from two years prior was set to make his mark on the AHL. MacDonald had a career year, recording the most goals by a defenseman (twenty), most points by a defenseman (fifty-five), being named an AHL All-Star, and named to the AHL First All-Star Team at the end of the season. Each of these statistics saw him earn his highest totals he's had in a season. He also appeared in seventy-five games.

"I've always worked to get what I want. You obviously try to get better and make it to the NHL." In the 2018 off-season, the Florida Panthers (yes, they make an appearance yet again!) signed MacDonald to a two-year, two-way contract.

Coming into the preseason and into his first NHL training camp, it initially wasn't expected he'd make the Panthers' roster. However, after an injury to another defenseman and a product of his own play, he earned a spot on opening night. In his first NHL game, on the road against the Tampa Bay Lightning, he scored his first goal on his first shot against goaltender Andrei Vasilevskiy.

1-for-2.

"It was one of the coolest things I've ever done in my entire life. For me, the coolest part was having my family and friends there." Even in the heat of the best moment in one of the best days of his life, he didn't let his first goal get the best of him. "In the moment, you're focused on the game, you know. You've got another shift you have to go after, you can't just say alright… it's all done!" It's one of the best mind-sets that one could possibly have in a state of euphoria. "You've got $#!% to take care of so it took a little while for that to finally hit home, but it's an amazing feeling, it really is."

It's a feeling that didn't just up-and-out, either. "You are just so happy that, honestly, I … it took me a couple of months just to realize that I had done that."

Though he turned heads and opened eyes after two games, one goal, and a plus one rating, he was loaned back to Spring-field, this time the Thunderbirds, for the rest of the 2018–19 season. "The Cats decided an additional full season in the American Hockey League would help complete Jacob Mac-Donald's overall development. Once again, MacDonald would display flashes of brilliance at the AHL level for the Thunderbirds," said Florida Panthers' Fansided writer, Sam Golub, noting that Panthers management felt he needed to develop more defensively.[41]

His plus/minus in the AHL increased from negative twen-ty-six in 2017–18 to negative two in 2018–19, signaling improvement as a two-way defenseman, albeit the offensive capabilities are certainly still there. MacDonald posted four-teen goals and twenty-nine assists in seventy-two AHL games this past season. It wasn't the same season statistically as 2017–18, but like I said earlier, you have to look beyond what you see on paper.

On June 29, 2019, the Colorado Avalanche acquired defen-seman Jacob MacDonald from the Florida Panthers for for-ward Dominic Toninato. Shortly after the trade was made, MacDonald posted to his Instagram a picture of a young kid, holding up an Avalanche jersey that was clearly too big.

---

41 Golub, Sam. 2019. "Florida Panthers: Jacob Macdonald Deserves An NHL Role". The Rat Trick.

However, the smile on the kid's face was priceless, stretching from ear to ear. Pure joy.

The caption read, "I am beyond excited to say that I get the chance to live my childhood dream with the @coloradoavalanche this upcoming season. Thank you to Florida for everything you've given me, I can't wait to get the season going."[42] He didn't get drafted by his favorite team, but he's now gotten a chance to play on that team. And, he's already got his first NHL game and first NHL goal both under his belt.

He's got a shot this season to join a very young team set to make strides in the big league, though he is starting the year with the Avalanche's recent ECHL-now AHL affiliate, the Colorado Eagles. It'll be interesting to see how things shake up for the *relatively* local guy.

---

42   MacDonald, Jacob. 'Traded to Avalanche." Instagram. June 29, 2019.

CHAPTER 7

JOSH CURRIE

———

Date of Birth: October 29, 1992

Birthplace: Charlottetown, Prince Edward Island, Canada

Position: Right Wing

Statistics to Note:

Year	Team	League	Games Played	Goals	Assists	Total Points	Penalty Minutes	Plus/ Minus
2011–2012	Prince Edward Island Rocket	QMJHL	68	30	16	46	33	-22
2012–2013	Prince Edward Island Rocket	QMJHL	68	49	55	104	62	26
2013–2014	Atlanta Gladiators	ECHL	70	15	16	31	41	-21
2014–2015	Bakersfield Condors	ECHL	71	14	28	42	49	-20
2015–2016	Norfolk Admirals	ECHL	13	6	6	12	8	-3
	Bakersfield Condors	AHL	53	10	14	24	49	8
2016–2017	Bakersfield Condors	AHL	67	22	14	36	28	-4
2017–2018	Bakersfield Condors	AHL	68	20	26	46	52	3
2018–2019	Edmonton Oilers	NHL	21	2	3	5	2	2
	Bakersfield Condors	AHL	53	27	14	41	17	6

43

Josh Currie didn't bother giving the ECHL a fleeting thought when he came off of an explosive 2012–13 year in the Quebec Major Junior Hockey League (QMJHL). His eyes were set on an NHL contract. After all, he had recorded forty-nine goals and fifty-five assists that year while holding the "C" for the now defunct Prince Edward Island Rocket, totaling 104 points—a fifty-eight-point jump from the previous year. He was, like MacDonald, named to his league's First All-Star Team.

---

43 "Elite Prospects - Josh Currie." Elite Prospects, 2019.

That NHL contract didn't come. Instead, he signed a contract with the AHL's Portland Pirates. "When I first signed with Portland, I was excited but also a little disappointed that I wasn't signing an NHL contract after such a successful overage campaign in PEI." He was surprised. "In the Rocket I played against players that signed NHL contracts and we had similar stats so I was very hopeful for an NHL contract."

The AHL is still just one level below the NHL, though. But, as the 2013–14 year started, he didn't make the Pirates out of training camp, and instead was sent down to their ECHL affiliate, the Gwinnett Gladiators. "I never even passed a thought about the ECHL, I really just thought I would be in the AHL." It was like he had suddenly just hit a brick wall.

It wasn't surprising to him that he was sent down to this level, it was actually straight disbelief. "At the time of being sent down I saw it as a demotion rather than a step of development. I really did not want to play in the ECHL as I felt I was able to play in the AHL. That was a tough pill to swallow."

Once that pill was swallowed, he received encouragement from others despite what he felt was unfair circumstances, but vowed to keep working at his play.

Currie had a modest fifteen goals and sixteen assists in seventy games in his first ECHL season, leading his team in games played, but it wasn't the season he was looking for. In the 2014 off-season, he'd sign with the Bakersfield Condors, another ECHL team at the time, who were owned by the Edmonton Oilers.

In the Condors' press release of a few signings, Currie said, "I'm looking at this season in Bakersfield as a fresh start for me. I want to build off the experience and season I had last year. I was able to learn the expectations of being a pro and know that I need to focus as much defensively as offensively."[44]

The 2014–15 season was an improvement over the previous season, with him scoring fourteen goals and twenty-eight assists in seventy-one games, while also working on shaping out his overall game. He led Bakersfield in scoring. Bakersfield's time as an ECHL team didn't last, though, as the Edmonton Oilers elected for the team to become the new AHL affiliate, displacing the ECHL team and relocating to Norfolk; Currie decided to go along and signed in Norfolk during the off-season. However, that move didn't last too long, either. As of the first thirteen games of the 2015–16 ECHL season, Currie amassed six goals and six assists in thirteen games earning a professional tryout (PTO) from none other than the AHL's Bakersfield Condors.

---

44 "Kremyr, Currie, And Little Agree To Terms". 2014. Bakersfieldcondors.Com.

"I definitely feel that playing in Bakersfield in the coast the year prior did play a role in being called up by them. JF Houle who was my head coach in ECHL Bakersfield also became the assistant with the AHL club and we had some history together, as he coached against me in the QMJHL for four years and we also got along really well during our time together in the ECHL." Currie continued, "JF had seen me play for quite a few years in the QMJHL and he knew what I could do. He believed that I could play in the AHL." Currie ran with the chance, with the help of his former coach.

He had a successful first year in the AHL, scoring ten goals and adding fourteen helpers in fifty-three games. This earned him another professional contract in January following the PTO, and then yet another from Bakersfield in June.[45] In another Condors press release, they described Josh as, "one of the team's leading penalty killers," which was a huge step in the right direction in making himself an all-around two-way forward. He also tied for the team lead in plus/minus.

In his fourth professional year, his numbers improved yet again to twenty-two goals and fourteen assists in sixty-seven games, earning—you guessed it—another AHL contract. This contract was a two-year AHL deal.[46] He was second on

---

45 "Currie Signs AHL Contract". 2016. Bakersfieldcondors.Com.
46 "CONDORS SIGN CURRIE AND O'BRIEN". 2017. Bakersfieldcondors.Com.

the team in goals, despite leading the team in shots with 156. He was also becoming a household name with the Condors, after playing a combined 191 games between the AHL and ECHL within the organization.

As the fifth season came around, he had another improved year, scoring twenty goals and adding twenty-six assists in sixty-eight games, finally earning himself in the off-season the much elusive NHL contract from the parent club, the Edmonton Oilers on a two-way, two-year deal. Relief, but work still to be done. As a kid, he had said, "I am going to play in the NHL," and he was just within reach.

Currie did not make the Oilers out of training camp, but became an alternate captain in Bakersfield as the season started. Currie had twenty-four goals and thirteen assists in forty-nine games to start the season for the Condors, and in his sixth professional season, he was called up to the big club—the Edmonton Oilers—on February 18, 2019. "I played against a lot of guys that are in the NHL so I fully understood what was needed to get there. I was so close, I just kept working and trying.....and then finally ...the call...'you're going up...' "

Five days later, on February 23, 2019, history was made as the tenured minor league player got a loose puck out of a scramble in front of the Anaheim Ducks' net, and banged home his first NHL goal, past former ECHL goaltender Kevin Boyle. An iconic Oilers goal horn sounded as 18,347 people cheered.[47]

"It was a feeling of unbelievable excitement and relief. It was what I have been working for all these years. It was a long journey coming up through the minors but I don't think I would've made it if it wasn't for my time in the ECHL." Though originally the ECHL wasn't even given a thought for him, it proved to be one of the best things that could have happened.

"The long, hard path tested my patience for sure but never my desire to get there," Currie went on. The capital of Prince Edward Island, Charlottetown, was up late at night eagerly hoping for a goal, and all went to bed happy as Currie became only the twelfth player from the small Canadian city to score their first NHL goal.

On April 5, 2019, he was returned to Bakersfield just in time for the Condors' end of the season and playoffs. However, he made his mark on the Rogers Place ice surface for the time being, recording a modest two goals and three assists over twenty-one games, despite logging fourth-line minutes at an average of eight minutes and forty-three seconds on ice per

47 "Anaheim Ducks At Edmonton Oilers Box Score — February 23, 2019". 2019. Hockey-Reference.Com.

night. A far cry from the twenty to thirty minutes per night that are often seen at the ECHL level.

This season will be his seventh professional season, and he's on the verge of cracking the Oilers' lineup on a more regular basis than the quarter of the season he played last year.

Of course, the dream and the ultimate goal is to be a full-time NHL player, but that has yet to be seen. "I am my own hardest critic. I know when I am not on my game or when things are just not clicking and I just dig deeper to play how I know I can. You have to learn when one game is over no matter how successful or unsuccessful you were, you need to park it and move on to preparing for the next game." You learn and you move forward.

The 2018–19 season was successful in many regards for Currie, but one thing is for certain: He's already put the season in the past and is striving for his next season of NHL action. And like his 2012–13 self, he's eyeing another NHL contract in the near future.

CHAPTER 8

SEAN DAY

———

Date of Birth: January 9, 1998

Birthplace: Leuven, Belgium → Dual Citizenship w/Canada

Position: Defense

Statistics to Note:

Year	Team	League	Games Played	Goals	Assists	Total Points	Penalty Minutes	Plus/ Minus
2013–2014	Mississauga Steelheads	OHL	60	6	10	16	34	-35
2014–2015	Mississauga Steelheads	OHL	61	10	26	36	62	-27
2015–2016	Mississauga Steelheads	OHL	57	6	16	22	27	-13
2016–2017	Mississauga Steelheads	OHL	5	3	2	5	4	4
	Windsor Spitfires	OHL	58	12	20	32	20	11
2017–2018	Windsor Spitfires	OHL	27	4	17	21	8	1
	Kingston Frontenacs	OHL	23	1	25	26	4	-11
2018–2019	Hartford Wolf Pack	AHL	46	3	11	14	8	-23
	Maine Mariners	ECHL	19	4	11	15	6	4

48

There's this weird rule in the Canadian Hockey League (CHL) called the "exceptional status" rule. According to Prospectpedia, exceptional status refers to "A player granted exceptional player status by Hockey Canada, enabling them to play a full season at 15 years old."[49]

To this day, there have been only a few players granted exceptional status. Most players begin CHL play at the ripe age of sixteen, but this isn't the case for a select handful. You may have heard of the first three:

---

48 "Elite Prospects - Sean Day." Elite Prospects, 2019.
49 Site no longer exists as of October, 2019.

John Tavares, Aaron Ekblad, and Connor McDavid.

All three were taken first overall in their respective draft classes, deservedly so, though some believe Ekblad shouldn't have gone first in retrospect (without a doubt still a top-tier pick).

You get the point, though. These three players are household names in the sport of ice hockey. And, quite frankly, are exceptional. Were exceptional in their junior ranks, as well.

The fourth, though, to be granted exceptional player status by Hockey Canada is Sean Day. His name doesn't exactly give the same ring as the first three.

So, who?

Day, at the early age of fourteen when given the exceptional status, as many suggested, was destined for NHL stardom. After all, exceptional status—especially to the OHL—is no small feat. In some ways, it's almost as if two words are supposed to define someone's career. Even, at age fourteen.

However, there were also others that didn't believe the hype.

Over the course of his Ontario Hockey League (OHL) career, the defenseman had put up 158 points over 291 regular season games. Respectable, but not exceptional. A staggering negative seventy plus/minus rating didn't scream exceptional status, either. [50]

However, progression was being made, it seemed, on a seasonal basis, as his defensive play slowly bettered, as well as his offensive side—though that seemed to take a bit of a dip during the 2015–16 season. In 2015, there were several problems off the ice which saw him take leaves of absence for the 2015–16 season. They were not *him* being a problem, but rather having other problems beyond his control, which I will not delve into.

Day, on draft day in 2016, didn't breach the top five, the top ten, or even the first round. He fell out of the second round, and seemingly fell off the draft board.

Finally, he was drafted in round three, number eighty-one overall by the New York Rangers. Although this is still impressive to be drafted this high, especially in a draft class that saw Patrik Laine and Auston Matthews battle for the first overall pick, Day wouldn't be fighting his draft mates.

He'd be fighting his predecessors to OHL Exceptional Status: John Tavares, Aaron Ekblad, and Connor McDavid.

---

50   "Elite Prospects - Sean Day." Elite Prospects, 2019.

Day would spend the 2016–17 and 2017–18 seasons continuing his development in junior hockey, where it seemed that he was back on the right track.

It was in 2018, at the age of twenty, that he finally turned pro. I say "finally," like it was expected he'd be fresh for the start of a famous professional hockey career at eighteen years old.

Truthfully, he wasn't.

Day started the 2018–19 season in the AHL after failing to make an already lackluster New York Rangers defensive core out of training camp. He wasn't having as successful a start as one may have hoped, going pointless in his first six games, and also recording a horrendous negative seven plus/minus rating. The statistics weren't there, nor the confidence.

The New York Rangers reassigned him to the ECHL's Maine Mariners.

Head coach of the Maine Mariners, Riley Armstrong, had this to say about Day upon being sent down to Maine:

"What Hartford is looking for is the player to get ice time and be into situations they might not have seen at Hartford. For Sean Day, maybe Gilmour was running the power play, but that is usually Sean Day's spot. That's what he prefers. But he wasn't seeing the minutes." It was a territory for him that was relatively unknown. "So to grab him and really kind of let him run the power play, let him get out there a lot. And it's all about building confidence and when those players are in Hartford, they're not playing a lot or they're not being in the spots to kind of gain that confidence or build it, or score a goal, or get a little assist, your confidence can go downhill pretty quick."

He continued, "When a player comes, like Sean Day, it's about trying to build his confidence back up, kind of getting that little swagger back in his game a little bit and get him back to having a little bit of fun enjoying the game. So then when he goes back up to Hartford, he has his game."

I had the pleasure of watching the former "exceptional status," player on a frequent basis to start the year. Every Mariners home game, I had a glance at what, being a Rangers fan, I hoped was near in our future.

Day looked out of place in his time with the Mariners.

Not in a bad way, but in a *really* great way. I'll reiterate. He was the best ECHL player I saw *live* this past year. Even beating some of the Cincinnati Cyclones players, who stomped Maine in their only meeting last season, scoring seven goals in the first period. *THE FIRST PERIOD.*

I witnessed raw skill, seemingly effortless skating, accurate shooting, and the ability to move the puck free-flowingly from Day. He wasn't overly physical, but used his body at opportune times, as needed.

He had an edge to him, something you like to see in a prospect. But, he also kept his cool. He didn't run his mouth to officials, or play dirty.

It quickly became apparent to me that Day wouldn't be down with the Mariners for long. While it was mesmerizing to see a player of his caliber performing, it did make me wonder: Why is he down here?

From my eye, center ice seating if I may add, Day was far and away the best player on the ice every game, beside Brandon Halverson, the Mariners' starting goaltender at the time, whose back was probably hurting from carrying us.

However, there were many little things that I found to be troubling, especially as Curtis Joe notes in his evaluation of Day on EliteProspects, "His consistency and enthusiasm exhibited at the game's defining moments does seem to wane, and the pressure felt seems to impact his decision-making slightly."[51]

---

51   Joe, Curtis. 2015. "Elite Prospects - Sean Day." Elite Prospects.

I found this to be especially relevant on the power play, as there were more than a few instances that he'd try and make passes that didn't warrant a need for the pass to be made.

There were also times when he'd turn over the puck at inopportune times, especially breaking it out of the defensive zone. Joe adds to the end of his assessment that Day, "has yet to put it all together and prove that he can thrive in the driver's seat." This evaluation is from 2015, which is troubling to see the same problems still present, but answers why he's down at the ECHL level. To develop, work on righting his wrongs, and learn from his mistakes.

Day's talents in his short stint with the Mariners brought about more positives than negatives, though. In nineteen games with the Mariners, he put up four goals and eleven assists in nineteen games played, serving as an offensive catalyst for a team that needed scoring and offensive help. Day's efforts even resulted in an ECHL All-Star Game spot, though as he was recalled to Hartford of the AHL, he could not participate. Since being sent back up to Hartford, Day started to turn his season around with fourteen points in forty games.

It's still not exceptional, but he has potential, and I truly do believe that he has the tools to become a formidable NHL defenseman. It's just that those offensive and defensive tools need some time to develop and to be fine-tuned.

Coach Armstrong later said, "He's feeling really good about himself. He knows that he can play against guys that age coming out of junior hockey. So, I think that's what it mostly is about. And it's, with the coaching staff, it's about building a relationship with Sean that you can get the most out of them." Having that mutual trust is incredibly important. "And once you build that relationship and Sean can feel comfortable with me and I'm comfortable with him and we understand each other and the way that he plays and how I want him to play. I think it just feeds off of that you could tell by the point production he put up. And then also with the point production he got in the second half of the season in Hartford as well."

He shouldn't be compared to Tavares, Ekblad, or McDavid, though that will always be a topic of discussion. In a 2016 interview, he even went as far to say that, "Now that I look back on [the exceptional status], I think maybe it wasn't the best thing to do for my development, because now I don't even look at myself as that kind of player anymore. I just want to be known as another draft eligible—just a normal player. Looking back, I think I wasn't ready. I think I've had to catch up with what people thought I should be."[52]

.

52 Cox, Damien. 2016. "Steelheads' Day Opens Up About Life Off The Ice." Sportsnet.Ca.

Round three, number eighty-one overall, to the New York Rangers.[53]

It's now 2019, and Sean Day hasn't seen a regular season NHL game... yet. But, he's twenty-one now. He's had a full season of professional hockey under his belt, and will be looking to improve those numbers next year. He's projected to take on a bigger role for the Hartford Wolf Pack.

These are ridiculously high expectations for someone that is undeservedly scrutinized. And, for a talent who is still *just twenty-one years old.*

The fifth player to receive exceptional status, after Day, is Joe Veleno, who was drafted with the last pick of the first round in the 2018 NHL entry draft to a struggling Detroit Red Wings team. Only time will tell whether his jump from Drummondville of the Quebec Major Junior Hockey League (QMJHL) to Detroit's system will be successful, but based off of his numbers with the Voltigeurs this past year, it should be.

But, as you've read, stats on paper *aren't everything.*

---

53   "Elite Prospects - Sean Day." Elite Prospects, 2019.

PART 3

WHAT CAN WE LEARN FROM THE PLAYERS?

You've heard from the players, so what can we learn from their experiences?

CHAPTER 9

INCREASED PLAYING TIME

INCREASED OPPORTUNITIES

It should be obvious, right? More playing time is always a good sign. Whether you've been on the first line the entire year, or you've gradually been going up the lineup, coach rewards you with more playing time, and you love it. It's natural excitement.

The NHL and AHL both run by the standard four lines and three defensive pairs, with the addition of either a seventh defenseman or thirteenth forward.

In the ECHL, though, it's not like that. The mechanics of the game remain the same, but the amount of people in a lineup changes. Each team includes just eighteen players in their game-night lineups—ten forwards, six defensemen, and two goaltenders. So, instead of rotating four lines, there are only three lines, with an additional forward to be included in additional rotations.

As Shane Harper put it, "So there's only three forward lines, so you're typically gonna play almost 20 minutes at least. And if you're playing well, you can play close to 30. Typically, most first line forwards in the NHL and AHL play an absolute maximum of around 21-22 minutes per night, assuming that the game doesn't go into overtime."

If you're a player struggling in the AHL on the fourth line, you're probably not playing those twenty-one to twenty-two minutes. You might be playing ten to twelve. It's not a lot, especially if you're trying to develop as a prospect. Less playing time is less opportunity.

When a prospect gets dropped down to the fourth line, they're not getting the chance to succeed—often because they're in a situation in which they haven't run with a previous chance. But, when they get sent down to the ECHL, being a player on a line in a higher league, they get more time. Harper continues, "I mean, if I'm gonna play 10 minutes in the AHL and then, I can play 30 or almost 25 minutes in the ECHL, that's two and a half games that I just played compared to one AHL game."

With increased opportunity, you get another chance. You make progress and up your production, or you don't. There's no in between. "It's more time with the puck. It's more game situations. Everything is just more advanced. You're gonna develop quicker automatically. That's just how it is."

Just like in soccer, more touches are more of a benefit than less. It's as simple as that. Your skills advance as you take advantage of developing them.

For a player like Sean Day, who wasn't seeing reps on the power play in Hartford before being sent down to Maine, the opportunity for him was to be able to be a first pairing defenseman in regular situations, as well as the power play catalyst that his game revolves around. Being able to play minutes in a variety of situations was integral to his success at the ECHL level. As Maine coach Riley Armstrong said, "What Hartford's looking for is the player to get ice time and be into situations they might not have seen at Hartford."

* * *

For goaltenders, increased playing time is vital, too. Mark Allred of Black n Gold Hockey said in a recent June 2019 article, "Now I know many minor-pro teams have had the three-headed monster in goal in the past, but in my opinion, it's not a very good idea. Playing time is so important to developing netminders, and in a league that predominantly operates on a Friday to Sunday weekly game schedule, one goaltender may take a step back in his pro progression due to lack of playing time."[54]

Which is true. The more time that a goaltender is able to see in-game action, the more scenarios they can adapt to, and perform. This is to an extent, though, as goaltenders shouldn't be given a heavy workload if they're not ready for it.

The "three-headed monster" situation, apparent in some franchises' minor affiliates, is positive in the fact that these teams are typically winning.

Many young goalies in today's game must "pay their dues" at lower levels before getting their chance at the NHL level. In theory, it's better for a goaltender to see more games at a lower level than to sit behind the starter at a higher level.

For a goaltender like Connor LaCouvee, it became apparent that the more time he played in both the AHL and ECHL this past year, the better he got, and the faster he developed. In turn, his confidence also skyrocketed.

As we look ahead into the 2019–20 season, with LaCouvee signed with the Laval Rocket, the "three-headed monster"

54 Allred Jr., Mark. 2019. "NHL Free Agency: Bruins To Sign Goaltender For Minor-Pro Depth". BLACK N GOLD HOCKEY PODCAST.

emerges in Montréal's farm team. In fact, as of the beginning of the season, it's a four-headed monster. LaCouvee, Cayden Primeau, Charlie Lindgren, and Michael McNiven are all going to be battling for spots in Laval the entire season with McNiven and Lacouvee starting in the ECHL. The NHL roster is set with the Canadiens' NHL duo of Carey Price and Keith Kinkaid locked in.

Assuming Cayden Primeau is locked as one of the goaltenders, being one of Montréal's prized prospects, it leaves the situation foggy. Laval seemed to have no problems last year sending prospects to various ECHL teams, but it doesn't rectify the situation, as they don't actually have an ECHL affiliate. If an injury happens to one of Primeau or Lindgren, they do have choices in who they can call up. However, it wouldn't be beneficial to have three goaltenders up at this time.

Less playing time is less opportunity to develop, plain and simple.

CHAPTER 10

PHYSICAL AND MENTAL PREPAREDNESS

You can't come into a preseason, out of shape and not ready for the year that is your career, in hockey. While the off-season is your off time, you have to be on top of things both physically and mentally.

If you're not in shape, it's a hard climb uphill trying to compete to the best of one's ability.

* * *

Coming out of the junior or college ranks, players never get the full seventy-two game ECHL schedule before coming in.

Let alone the eighty-two game NHL schedule. Or the AHL schedule, at seventy-six games, in the middle.

Jacob MacDonald said, "If you can't keep up, you're not going to make it very far." No truer words have been said. As much as one may possess individual skill or talent, endurance and stamina are driving factors in the ability to continuously compete. With the ability to continuously compete comes another factor of keeping your body in shape.

He continued, "It's really taking care of your body and making sure you're ready to go for every single game, and working out in a little bit of a different manner, where you don't necessarily have to focus on being, bulky and strong and heavy in the corners and all that. It's more about speed and the pro game right now, is so much speed-based." He talked how in college, you'd get run into the endboards if you took too long with the puck, or even if you gave it up.

With a change in the game style, changing the body type can work its advantages as well. You start to not get run into the endboards every time you're behind the net.

It still happens from time to time, but not *every time* you collect the puck from behind your net.

What he's conveying is that you can adjust how you train based on the style of game that is played by you, your teammates, and your league.

Josh Currie had more of the same to say: "I was able to adapt and learn how to play against full grown men who were much stronger than I was at the time. It also showed me that I needed to get stronger and faster... I learned how to eat properly and take care of my body properly. I could see that this was a full time job and I needed to work at it every day of the week."

It is a full-time job—both the hockey part, and physically taking care of yourself. A body requires constant maintenance in sports. Hockey isn't the only sport. In football, baseball, or basketball, the point remains the same. You have to be able to compete, but also take care of yourself.

Evidently, the results of taking care of your body are fruitful. You learn as much about yourself as what it is to be a professional, and what's expected as said professional. It helps during performance on the ice, and also helps the mental side of the game.

* * *

You probably know the sayings about the mental fortitude of goalies. I really like the one that goes, "Half the game is mental. The other half is being mental."

Whoever first said that, they're not wrong. Being a goaltender myself, I can attest to us being a different breed. Honestly, who in their right mind thinks that trying to stop small vulcanized rubber projectiles from going into a four by six-foot net is fun?

We do.

And, so it goes. Such is life.

The ECHL is often one of the first places that a player plays in professionally—though a league like the Southern Professional Hockey League often gets a lot of players as well that are just making their jump to pro hockey, but aren't quite at the ECHL's pace.

While the physical preparedness of playing at a higher level is of the utmost importance, mental preparedness is just as, if not equally, important.

As you've read previously with Connor LaCouvee, his mind set hasn't changed since making the jump to pro hockey, despite the variety of good and bad hands that he's been dealt. For some, the adversity in which he's faced is already too much. Being told that they're just going to be a backup at the AHL level while the starter rehabs an injury, or that they're the third-string goaltender going into a season, it may have them question what their potential really is.

But keeping the mind-set to play and prepare like it's their job, and that they can succeed, is incredibly important. Having the right mind-set is crucial to any player's focus.

Josh Currie said, "I know when I am not on my game or when things are just not clicking and I just dig deeper to play how I know I can. You have to learn when one game is over no matter how successful or unsuccessful you were, you need to park it and move on to preparing for the next game. It is easy to get in your own head. I call my parents after almost every game, discuss it and then move on. You need to evaluate your part and look forward. That is tough sometimes. On several teams I have been termed the 'workhorse' and I guess I can see that."

Workhorse, in this regard, is a total mental term. You learn, and you move on. You talk, and you realize what was done wrong. You learn from your successes, as much as you learn from your failures.

Ted Monnich, a sport psychology consultant who works primarily with goaltenders, said in a 2016 article, "It's not easy to face our failures, and even harder to accept our weaknesses. But everyone has weaknesses. Our culture tends to view weaknesses as negative and to be avoided. As such, we don't face our weaknesses, and we keep falling to them."[55]

55 Monnich, Ted. 2016. "Monnich's Mental Game: Turning Goaltending Failure Into Success." Ingoal Magazine.

This is exactly what players need to avoid, regardless of being a goaltender or skater.

Mental preparedness is sometimes dictated by physical preparedness, as well. Jacob MacDonald had this to say, combining the physical and mental sides:

"When you wake up on Sunday and you're playing your third game in 3 days, you really gotta mentally dial yourself into that because switching from the two games a weekend format [in college], you're getting ready to call it for the weekend. That's when you dial yourself in for when you wake up on Sunday, and you have a game to play."

He followed with an example: "I think it was the second weekend of being in Elmira, we had a three in three, the last two weekends. I was only there for three weeks after my senior year, and it's like, 'yeah, I'm ready to go full energy,' but I'm looking around at the guys who are in 75 games a year... And they're all dead, and it's game 70 of the year, dead. And I'm just ready to go because I'm so excited."

After being excited the first time around, though, his mindset may have shifted a little after a few years.

"You know, I'm fresh out of college, and all these guys are dead, and after my fourth year just finished, I'm like yeah, I know exactly what the hell those guys are feeling."

The reason I say that this is a combination of mental and physical preparedness is that his mind set quite literally took a 180 after realizing the physical side that was so inherently present in playing more than just the college game, and more than just skipping Sunday's.

For prospects, it's a huge turn, mentally preparing to play seventy-two regular season games, and potentially playoff games. For goalies, it's not seventy-two games, but it's preparing to be ready to go and play any given night at any given time. A bad showing or a string of bad showings could lead a goalie onto the bench, and maybe even off the team, hurting their chances of 'making it' in upper tiers of professional hockey.

While I supported goaltender Ed Minney during his time with the Maine Mariners, it's exactly what happened. While it isn't necessarily because of mind set, though he appeared distraught from goals he gave in during his few appearances, a few bad games and he wound up off the team. He wasn't the solution, and he's back in the SPHL. However, in his time with Wichita, he posted a 1.63 GAA and .917 SV% over two appearances, which is promising for another chance in the future.[56]

For goaltender Connor LaCouvee, it was the exact opposite. A string of great showings led to a chance off the team, at a higher level, for which he earned a contract.

---

56 "Elite Prospects - Ed Minney." Elite Prospects, 2019.

CHAPTER 11

THE IMPORTANCE OF EXPERIENCE AND CONNECTIONS

———

Let's face it. Playing professionally is a privilege, given to those that have dedicated their time and worked hard at achieving certain goals. There have been tens of thousands of professional hockey players over the history of the sport.

Often getting a taste promotes a passion, warranting for the need for an experience.

Some will play over 1,000 games in the NHL. Others will become the journeyman in the AHL. Then, there are also players that will make their one ECHL appearance, only to never grace professional hockey ever again.

However, each of these players had an experience. While the experience is significantly longer for some than others, each player on the ice at any given time is part of a collective experience of their linemates, their coaches, their atmosphere, and the other team.

My point of writing something so cliché, is that in the "E," there are hundreds of players looking to improve their game, and make a name for themselves, to get noticed, and get better opportunities. They shift up and down lineups, get traded around like O-Pee-Chee cards in the spokes of bikes, and may get scratched here or there.

More often than not, playing in the ECHL does not lead to the NHL, and that's a simple fact. There have been 662 *total* alumni to reach the NHL since the league's inception in 1988. You may be sick of reading that, but it's a crucial statistic in understanding the past, present, and future of the league.

However, it does not deter the drive of its players to reach the AHL, and then the NHL.

At the AA level, it's all about fine tuning your game for a chance. That chance may come, or it may not. But, if one does *not* put in the effort, time, and dedication to singularly, "hockey," they would never be able to have that first chance at a chance.

Some players met in the context of professional hockey are content with simply playing professional hockey, and being paid for it. It's a way of extending their careers, or simply living out a childhood dream of being paid to play hockey while having fun and doing something that they love. These players may not be actively looking to move through the ranks to an NHL contract, but rather just, for the love of the game. They play because they love to play.

Or, perhaps, there is a player in the neutral ground. Who, if they played just one second in the NHL, they would "die happy." But, then there are the players who would certainly leave it all on the line to stay there.

These players, who make significant sacrifices by one way or another, are players that play because they want to get to that next level.

Jacob MacDonald stated, "If you want to get better, and you want to grow your game, and you want to continue to try to become the best hockey player you could be, which is my goal, as it should be for most people... I've only played two games in the NHL. So, for me, I know for a fact that I'm not at the highest level that I'm capable of, so that's why I'm continuing to try to become a better player every day, whether it's in season or out of season."

It's important to experience the professional side of the game, off the ice as well. Maine Mariners head coach Riley Armstrong said, "I think a lot of kids that come out of college hockey usually end up in the ECHL and then just from the past experiences last year we had Rangers' draft picks who are fairly young as well, 20-21 years old." Examples: Ty Ronning, Sean Day. "And I think it allows them to kind of develop being mature away from the rink. I think a lot of guys are really good hockey players, but now they're living on their own. They're not with a billet family and it's allowing them to grow up away from the rink. Whether that's cooking their own meals instead of just eating cereal for every meal, maybe venturing out to cooking chicken or steak for themselves. And it is a little bit of a learning curve for a lot of guys once they get into this position."

For some players new to the pro game, it's also about managing money. While MacDonald mentioned that players are playing for the love of the game, and not necessarily the financial side of things, it can't be overlooked. Players have a choice of what they do with their money. Are they going to buy a new pair of shoes, or are they going to tuck it away?

Armstrong credits older veteran guys that have been around the ECHL for a while in ensuring that things will go smoothly: "I think it's always important on every team to have a guy like Zach Tolkinen and Terrence Wallin, those older guys who who can kind of help the young guys and and you see at every level they always want to bring in like a good vet to help out in the locker room to kind of mentor the young guys. And some guys take longer than other guys that kind of make that learning curve and it's just the maturity level that guys grab a lot quicker than others." Tolkinen was the Mariners' inaugural "C" this past season, while Wallin was given an "A." Together, entering the season, they had combined for 443 ECHL games.[57] [58]

For young players, it's important to learn the professional roles on and off the ice, and it's important to learn from the experience and/or experiences of others.

* * *

For the vast majority of us nonprofessional and often beer-league hockey players, we go to work part-time or full-time, go to college, or find ourselves playing 'chel with the boys on a Tuesday night.

---

57 "Elite Prospects - Zach Tolkinen." Elite Prospects, 2019.
58 "Elite Prospects - Terrence Wallin." Elite Prospects, 2019.

I think I do a pretty good job of setting the scene. It's you. It's me. Let's face the reality.

Ever since high school, I've been taught the importance of connections. In fact, in my freshman year of college, I was on the LinkedIn train, ready to add more connections. Every person I meet, I see if they're on there immediately after.

It's the Facebook for grown-ups, it seems.

And with every connection, I open a new door or a new pathway with someone I previously hadn't followed, which puts me in their web and them in mine.

At one of the Maine Mariners games earlier this season, the Stanley Cup came to town. And, so did the Keeper of the Cup, Phil Pritchard.

If you know hockey, you know Phil Pritchard. After taking my picture with Lord Stanley, I made sure to go up and talk to Phil for a while. Also there was a guy I had never seen before, or even known.

It was Mario Della-Savia, another Keeper of the Cup. And he, like Phil, was passionate about hockey, wide-eyed, and eager to hear what I had to say, while we shared a few laughs.

You bet, I immediately reached out to connect with him, and he accepted. It's the little things like this. They may or may not materialize into anything, and I'm okay with that. But, I made the effort to connect.

Professional hockey players also thrive on connections. Josh Currie, while in Bakersfield in the ECHL, was able to get another opportunity at the AHL level, partly due to a previous connection. "I definitely feel that playing in Bakersfield in the coast the year prior did play a role in being called up by them. JF Houle who was my head coach in ECHL Bakersfield also became the assistant with the AHL club and we had some history together, as he coached against me in the QMJHL for four years and we also got along really well during our time together in the ECHL." He continued, "JF had seen me play for quite a few years in the QMJHL and he knew what I could do. He believed that I could play in the AHL."

For Shane Harper, when he got dropped into Trenton's ECHL program, it was a rough patch, almost like he wasn't having fun. But, with a new coach, Vinny Williams, things changed. His coach saw the potential in him. "He dropped me right into the line-up. He played me a lot, put me on the power play, and I just kind of thrived as soon as I got there and it was kinda like hockey was fun again." Harper would later, in 2013–14, sign a deal with the Orlando Solar Bears of the ECHL. Williams was the coach. However, Harper then signed a deal with the Chicago Wolves of the AHL, which voided that. But the connection was there in a worst-case, fall-back scenario.

Connor LaCouvee's situation was different, as a reach-out changed the face of the year. Riley Armstrong contacted him directly, just saying the Mariners were interested in him. That's all.

Nothing more than a simple reach-out and a new connection—someone he did not have a history with, shaped his first pro year.

And, how can we forget about Jacob MacDonald? His coach, Jamie Russell, he had met from Cornell, as Russell had coached Cornell years before.

"When I got the call from Elmira from a guy who I had met in the past, because he coached in Cornell before - so I had met him before - I was a little bit more familiar with him… it made the decision really easy for me… Once I was ready to go, I was down in Elmira, so he made it really easy."

The overarching point being: Connections are crucial. And developing them allows players to develop not only on the ice, but as a professional off the ice as well.

PART 4

DEVELOPING THROUGH AN ORGANIZATION

Developing the developmental side of things? Get it? I hope so.

CHAPTER 12

A MODEL DEVELOPMENTAL TEAM— THE NEWFOUNDLAND GROWLERS

—

The Newfoundland Growlers are an expansion team whose inaugural 2018–19 season saw them take the league by storm, having finished second in the Eastern Conference to the Florida Everblades in the regular season, and ultimately winning the league's championship trophy, the Kelly Cup.

They frustrated a lot of people along the way, utilizing a variety of players on AHL-ECHL two-way contracts. But, at the end of the day, they're winners, and there were twenty-six losers. In doing so, they also developed a plethora of younger players along the way. So, it shouldn't be surprising who they're affiliated with. The AHL team has had nothing but great successes in recent years, and with the NHL team's emphasis on their ECHL teams, it's no surprise.

They're affiliated with the Toronto Marlies and Toronto Maple Leafs.

Kyle Dubas, general manager of the Toronto Maple Leafs, had many positives to say about the Growlers, and shared his thoughts about what should be the norm in professional hockey. Robin Short of *The Telegram* summarized it as, "he'd like to see his organization aligned in the same vein as baseball's minor leagues, with players breaking into AA ball (ECHL), before climbing to AAA (American Hockey League) and perhaps, down the road, to the big leagues (NHL)." Dubas, in his words, said, "We want to use (the Growlers) for everybody entering the organization … players, coaches, trainers and medical people. We want a close connection throughout the entire organization. We want it all aligned."[59]

---

59 Short, Robin. 2019. "A Good Start As A Starting Point: Newfoundland Growlers Doing 'A Great Job,' Says Maple Leafs' GM Kyle Dubas." Thetelegram.Com.

The Leafs had done a decent job of this when they had an ECHL affiliation with the Orlando Solar Bears, but it hasn't taken off like this has.

Staying completely aligned means that the players in the minors use the same in-game systems as those above them, and that transitioning from each league, players already know what's expected, how they should play, positional queues, and so on. It means that everything runs smoothly. Everything comes and goes without a hitch. A call-up or send down won't, or at least shouldn't, exhibit many systematic problems. It is a mind-set.

It's not just players, either. Coaches, trainers, medical staff, and even in-arena sales, marketing, and public relations specialists all must start somewhere. The Maple Leafs are branding their name so that it flows through the minors, and that everyone knows—the Growlers are some of the future of the Leafs. It may not be apparent now, or next year. Heck, some of the players from this year's Kelly Cup-winning team may never don the blue and white. But, the thought is there. And plenty of them will certainly end up playing for the AHL affiliate, giving bona fide AHL talents competition.

Baseball is a great example of how minor league systems work—each team relies on their prospects being developed at a lower level, working their way to a higher level, and ultimately reaching the big leagues. A player must prove themselves at every level, but once they're in the big leagues, the prospect development course has done its job.

Some prospects could potentially climb the ladder throughout the year for their chance.

Even at the beginning of last season, the expectations were already in place for then head coach and former NHL veteran Ryane Clowe, to use the Growlers as a pipeline for the Marlies and Maple Leafs. A Maple Leafs staff writer wrote in a June 2018 article, "In his new position, Clowe will work closely with the Maple Leafs development staff and receive personnel support from the Maple Leafs hockey operations staff as the Growlers open their inaugural season in October of 2018. He is slated to attend the Maple Leafs development camp next week as well as training camp with the Maple Leafs and Marlies in September."[60]

While Clowe has since stepped down from the head coaching position, expectations are still the same for the still relatively new ECHL franchise. Six players on the Growlers from this past season had attended the Maple Leafs' prospect development camp last year, and it's expected that several players

---

60 Staff Writer. "Ryane Clowe Named Head Coach Of Newfoundland
    Growlers." 2018. NHL.Com.

from this year's camp should find themselves on the roster as well.

Many other ECHL teams are likely to see a few prospects from the NHL hit their ranks, but it's not to the extent at which the Maple Leafs organization is streamlining the development. Many NHL teams affiliated with ECHL clubs often have deals in place that sends an NHL-contracted goaltending prospect down, and not necessarily a player.

This makes complete sense, as NHL teams typically have four plus contracted goaltenders at any given time. Some teams have as many as six, and two goaltenders may be on an ECHL team at the same time. It doesn't stunt either goaltender's development, and the competition is embraced.

There's an expectancy that because of the plethora of signed goaltenders, Newfoundland could see the likes of either or perhaps two of the Leafs' high-profile goaltenders, Joseph Woll or Ian Scott. However, with Scott injured to start the season, and Woll at the AHL level, it's unclear if that will happen.

Michael Garteig, the Growlers' starting goaltender from this past year, is off to Finland. Mario Culina is off to USports. The Growlers are currently using Patrick Munson, who played in the EIHL last year, and Maxim Zhukov, a former Vegas

Golden Knights draft pick. But when Ian Scott comes back from injury, it's likely we'll see a third goalie join the fray.

Like their rivals, the Montréal Canadiens, Toronto's depth in goaltending is plentiful, but spots in the AHL are not.

As for skaters, the Growlers' roster only contains seven ECHL-contracted players, which signals to everyone that the Leafs and Marlies will have a heavy hand in filling out the rest of their roster. Any player cut by the Leafs and/or the Marlies will most likely be seeing time in the ECHL with Newfoundland. In turn, the Growlers should have another well-rounded roster for their second year.

Like it or not, it's been proven successful through last year to go this route and have a heavy influx of AHL players developing in the ECHL.

CHAPTER 13

THE STAGNANT NUMBERS

In May, I reached out to the Professional Hockey Players' Association (PHPA) in trying to schedule some interviews with former ECHL players. At first, I thought it was a bit of a long shot. College kid, weird request, weird book project... You know how it is.

If you're unfamiliar with the PHPA, here is a segment taken directly from the *About* section found on their website:

The Professional Hockey Players' Association is the certified, US National Labor Relations Board collective bargaining representative for all professional hockey players within the American Hockey League (AHL) and ECHL. As the only minor league Players' Association within a major league sport, the PHPA is one of the largest Players' Associations within the professional sports industry, boasting approximately 1,600 Members situated across 58 teams throughout North America.

While the Association has many functions, the primary function of the PHPA is to negotiate Player benefits by way of a Collective Bargaining Agreement (CBA). These benefits include: health and welfare benefits, training camp allowances, travel and trade relocation expenses, daily per diem, housing allowances, playoff shares, licensing rights, revenue-sharing, and Membership Assistance Programs.

With salaries of PHPA Members, to a great extent being pre-determined by each Member's previous play or value to an organization, the PHPA is focused on enhancing the membership's quality of life while they pursue their dream. As such, the Association's mission statement captures this characteristic...

The Professional Hockey Players' Association, through superior preparedness and experience, is committed to the enhancement and protection of Players' rights, as its Members pursue advancement in the sport of professional hockey.[61]

---

61   "About The PHPA." 2019. Phpa.Com.

The organization is as professional as they come, and has long since its inception garnered a very positive image while representing thousands of professional hockey players and their dreams.

To my surprise, as I sent in my first email inquiry reaching out to the PHPA, I was immediately sent a response from Darryl Dionne, Director of Marketing, Communications, and Business Development. He was polite, informative, communicated clearly, and helped my odd business. What more could you ask for?

Over the next few days, we exchanged messages and through his help, I was able to schedule my first interview and then a few after.

At around the same time that Darryl and I were exchanging emails, Randy Wilson, also of the PHPA, learned of my book and sent me a link to a very interesting article about the Maple Leafs, Kyle Dubas, and their relationship with their ECHL affiliate, the Newfoundland Growlers. It was an article that began to pick up steam immediately after being published.

This article is well written, informative, and puts into perspective a more analytical view of how the ECHL is as a developmental league in the present. I had to add this article, as it's one of the best pieces of writing surrounding the ECHL that I've read to date.

Katya Knappe, the author of this article, did some digging and threw together this chart showing ECHL players by age over the course of the past five years' time (via Elite Prospects).

For clarity, '18-19' refers to the 2018-19 season, and 'GP' refers to games played. '17-18' refers to the 2017-18 season, and so on.

Age	18–19	18–19 - 20+ GP	17–18	17–18 - 20+ GP	16–17	16–17 - 20+ GP	15–16	15–16 - 20+ GP	14–15	14–15 - 20+ GP
U19	1	0	0	0	0	0	1	0	1	0
U20	4	0	3	0	1	0	3	1	1	0
U21	42	14	47	11	38	13	36	17	42	12
U22	119	61	114	58	109	54	117	59	111	62
U23	200	105	192	103	193	108	206	114	210	119
O30	58	36	56	39	51	39	55	42	59	45
Total	1029	634	1010	634	952	620	978	650	984	650

62

Unfortunately, this is where the word "stagnant" comes into play. While there is an increasing amount of ECHL alumni going on to play more in the AHL, NHL, and other professional leagues, there is relatively no growth in younger players entering the league as prospects within the past five years. *This is a problem.*

---

62 Knappe, Katya. 2019. "Have Kyle Dubas And The Leafs Turned The ECHL Into A Development League For NHL Players?" Pension Plan Puppets.

But, as Knappe goes on, the Growlers are doing things differently, right?

Here are the nine U22 players that appeared for the Growlers this season, as well as their regular season statistics:

Giorgio Estephan - 6th round pick of the Sabres, signed to an AHL deal as a FA [Free Agent]

Matt Bradley - 5th round pick of the Canadiens, signed to an AHL deal as a FA

Ryan Moore - undrafted FA signing on an AHL deal

Kristians Rubins - undrafted FA signing from CHL [Canadian Hockey League] (Sweden before that) was on an ECHL deal, was upped to an AHL contract recently

Tate Olson - 7th round pick of the Canucks, acquired in a trade with another ECHL team, traded to the Everblades, went to U Sports [Canadian collegiate ice hockey / Canada's Division I]

Maxim Mizyurin - undrafted from CHL (Russia before that), was on a try-out deal, did not play after release

Hudson Elynuik - 3rd round pick of the Hurricanes, signed to an AHL deal as a FA

Semyon Der Arguchintsev - Leafs draft pick, NHL contract (post OHL season assignment)

Timothy Liljegren - Leafs draft pick, NHL contract (rehab assignment).[63]

Player	Games Played	Goals	Assists	Plus/Minus
Giorgio Estephan*	69	20	33	-2
Matt Bradley	66	15	30	11
Ryan Moore	50	11	14	-5
Kristians Rubins	56	2	16	17
Tate Olson	5	0	1	-2
Maxim Mizyurin	6	1	0	-1
Hudson Elynuik**	33	9	19	3
Semyon Der Arguchintsev	3	1	1	-1
Timothy Liljegren	1	0	0	0

*Estephan had 24 points in 23 games in the playoffs.

**Elynuik had 15 points in 16 games in the playoffs. [64]

I was actually in attendance for the one game that Liljegren was on for the rehab assignment. Like Sean Day, who was talked about in a chapter earlier, he looked totally out of place, and for all the right reasons. His skating was effortless. It looked like he wasn't even trying. He probably wasn't, for that matter. A rehab assignment is a rehab assignment.

Statistically, five of those players in the chart above put up impressive baseline numbers. Der Arguchintsev also put up

63 Ibid.
64 "Elite Prospects - 2018-19 Newfoundland Growlers." Elite Prospects, 2019.

respectable numbers, but inevitably will play back in the OHL this season. The others have legitimate shots at seeing AHL time and competing for higher roster spots than in New-foundland this season, though Newfoundland would be a good team to fall back on.

The U22 prospects aren't the only ones, though. Players like Brady Ferguson, twenty-four, are expected to make more of an AHL impact after posting fifty-eight points in forty-nine regular season games and twenty-four points in twenty-three playoff games.

And then, there's a guy like Zach O'Brien, who has just turned twenty-seven after the season ended. He's bounced between the ECHL and AHL since 2013, but exploded this year for sixty-eight points in fifty-three regular season ECHL games. Even at age twenty-seven, there's still a chance for him to climb the ladder.

Knappe then goes on to say:

What the Growlers can do, with their high number of young players, Europeans and players on AHL deals, is help change the ECHL from a bash and crash league into one where you don't fear for the health of your developing players. Ryan Crelin, the new Commissioner of the ECHL, said he wants that image to change in an interview at a Growlers game. But just saying something is different doesn't mean it actually is. And so far, this much talked about new development model doesn't look very different from the old.[65]

I really want to focus in on this quote here. Because, frankly, I do agree with Knappe. And, this is where the article shifts in the direction that I'm pinpointing.

While we want to see the change from the "bash and crash league," which the ECHL to some extent has been for the entirety of its existence, to a more fluid and safer league much like the NHL, it's not 100 percent where it needs to be.

While I will forever stand by my statement that the ECHL is a true developmental league for NHL-caliber players—and there's really no denying that, there is a lot of room for change in the league itself. A lot of room to "develop" the developmental model that has been put forth through the Leafs' system.

The developmental model is in place, and is set forth—I believe—near perfectly by the Newfoundland Growlers who have allowed an influx of younger players to gain experience, as well as give those who were not getting playing time in the

---

65   Knappe, Katya. 2019. "Have Kyle Dubas And The Leafs Turned The ECHL Into A Development League For NHL Players?" Pension Plan Puppets.

AHL, playing time in the ECHL. Of course, their affiliated teams play a large role in allowing that to happen. And, as soon as those players start to perform at a higher rate than at which they were, they are allowed AHL opportunities as seen fit by the AHL and NHL clubs, respectively.

But, it is incredibly evident that not every organization follows this developmental model. There are players that simply get scratched game after game in AHL organizations, that aren't set to the ECHL because a) the organization as a whole does not work closely with the ECHL team, b) there is not room for the player, or c) the organization doesn't *have* an ECHL affiliate.

Hear me out, though.

There were nine U22 players on the Growlers this season. Imagine that every ECHL team follows suit with their NHL affiliates. Twenty-five out of the twenty-six teams have AHL-NHL affiliations.

Imagine that each team is able to bring onto their ECHL club nine U22 players, like the Growlers have. It's not unachievable. Or even just eight. That's an additional 192 to 216 U22 players, which would completely turn the league into a more well-rounded developmental league with a heavy influx of younger talent. It would nearly double what the current amount of U22 players is, as well as add to the U23 totals substantially.

Yes, some players are going to be weeded out, and have to find new places to play. But, that's always been a part of the game. There's as much the game itself as the business side beside it.

What I am *not* saying is to eliminate players over the age of twenty-five. I'm all for thirty-six-year-old Jesse Schultz scoring over a point per game this past

season for Cincinnati. I'm all for twenty-seven-year-old Shane Harper getting his first NHL goal at that age. I'm all for having depth players fighting for their next chance at the AHL level, or veteran leaders in the locker room. It doesn't have to be a mass exodus.

There is no problem with having middle-aged (hockey-aged) players playing, but the number of them will most likely decline—slowly albeit—until there is a constant influx of younger players within the league.

But, think of it this way: Since the Vegas Golden Knights' expansion into the NHL, there have been 651 players selected in the NHL Entry Draft. That's 651 players over thirty-one teams that are in the process of being developed/ have been developed to the NHL level. Not all 651 players will be NHL players, and some may never make the AHL. But, with 217 plus new players in future entry drafts each year, these players need a place to go to develop. The ECHL is going to be that place when room in the AHL has reached its capacity.

There's one more point from Knappe's article I'd like to comment on, and it's this:

In terms of developing prospects, getting someone ready to play a depth role in the AHL isn't really all that important. And there is no evidence that an ECHL team is going to give you anything more than that. Despite what the Commissioner says, the ECHL had 49 players with over 100 PIM last year, and the AHL had 26. The ECHL had 16 players with between 10 and 20 fighting majors, while the AHL had one player with 10 because they have suspension rules to limit fighting. Teams routinely market their ECHL product on fights, truculence and grit. It's no place for the youngest prospects… I have to ask if it's a fit place for any prospect, no matter the image the league wants to promote.[66]

For one, depth roles are important in any professional team. And teams work in a ladder system. It's incredibly evident with goaltenders going 1–2, 3–4, 5–6. When goaltender 2 in the depth chart gets hurt, it usually then goes 1–3,4–5, 6. There is an organizational shift.

---

66   Ibid.

This same organizational shift happens with forwards and defensemen, but at a much lesser rate. As a player gets injured in the NHL, an AHL player is called up, and another AHL player gets a chance, which could in turn mean that an ECHL player gets recalled or loaned. When a trade is made, the same thing may potentially happen when there are multiple AHL players that suddenly get shifted into more playing time, or into a depth role at a higher level.

It's especially important to keep developing players even if just for a depth role, it *gives them a chance and an opportunity to run with.*

Secondly, there is no denying that the ECHL is still a rough league that is partially marketed on fighting and grit and that "bash and crash" style of play—as those two factors pull in tons of non hockey fans or casual fans. Filling the seats, as I'll talk about later, is very important to keep teams alive.

Talk to any little kid who knows nothing about hockey but sure as hell loves the games, and they'll mention the word "fight." I totally realize the importance of keeping players safe. It is of the utmost importance, especially for younger players.

But, at the same time, I would rather a younger player get acclimated to pro hockey at a lower level than a level that they are unprepared for like the AHL. They will still play the same age proportions, and as the league moves away from fighting and that style, they'll start to see more players close to their age.

Lastly, questioning the league as a "fit place for any prospect," is totally counterintuitive. Taking out the prospects is something that would be extremely detrimental to the league and the way that they're trying to go.

This stuff doesn't happen overnight. It takes years for changes to happen. And, while the change so far has been slow, teams are starting to pick up on the importance of placing their players or watching others develop in the ECHL, and that it is a league that could ultimately change face in containing and developing prospects, given ample time.

PART 5

WHAT CAN THE ECHL DO BETTER AS A DEVELOPMENTAL LEAGUE?

What can be done to enhance prospect development and player development? What changes can be made to more positively benefit the players?

CHAPTER 14

BETTER SCHEDULING AND FINANCIAL STABILITY

Through most of the players that I had talked to, it became apparent that the ECHL does need to do away with, or significantly reduce, the three in three types of weekends, or four games in five nights, especially if travel is involved. Josh Currie put it best, saying, "The league can be a grind as many players who have played in the league know. The ECHL can have some long and tough travel and you play lots of 3 and 3's or 4 games in 5 nights all while traveling on buses or sleeper buses," and Shane Harper added, "The only struggles, I guess, would be some of the travel, and if you ever have to play like, three games in three nights."

Changing that schedule is easier said than done, though. Harper made sure to point out that these schedules are also a product of people coming out to the games.

In the NHL, it's less of a worry having a game on a Tuesday night, even if it's a smaller market. You'll still get a decent sized crowd. But, at the ECHL level, a Tuesday night may be an empty arena. Wednesday night, same story. Need proof?

On Wednesday, February 13, 2019, the Maine Mariners took on the Worcester Railers, at home at the Cross Insurance Arena, in Portland, Maine. It had snowed a bit that day, but the roads weren't too bad—and if you've ever lived in Maine, you learn to accept the snow and go right through it.

Upon arrival, it didn't look like many were there, granted, I showed up about half an hour early. As game time came, the numbers didn't really change. In fact, there were so few people, that my friends and I could literally count every person in attendance—and I think we ended up with just shy of 250 people—staff included, players excluded. It was one of the best games of the season, with former Buffalo Sabres third round draft pick Brycen Martin sealing the deal on a 4–1 third period comeback in the first couple of minutes of overtime.

While having games almost exclusively on weekends and often in clusters is detrimental to the physical abilities of players, it keeps the league *alive*. People come on the weekends. People aren't working.

I believe that the best possible scenario would be to have three games in four nights, on Thursday, Saturday, and Sunday, using Friday as a travel and/or rest day. The two games on the weekends should ultimately be home and homes, or with another divisional team within close proximity. While Friday night is a great night for fans to go out and watch a game, having a Friday-Saturday-Sunday triple-header with an early Sunday game(often in the mid-afternoon) is *not* good for players.

Obviously, players will continue to persevere. This is their profession. But, it would also help players—especially later in the season—maintain health and physical readiness. Having games at 7:00 p.m. on Friday, 6:00 p.m. on Saturday, and 3:00 p.m. on Sunday, is simply too much.

Especially for younger players, who aren't acclimated to the length of a longer season—it's detrimental to their development, as they're being relied upon at least twenty to thirty minutes per night, and often find themselves on the brink of exhaustion by the end of a segment of games.

At the same time, as mentioned earlier, playing time and opportunities are integral in development. There's a fine line in determining to what extent a player can handle minutes.

Of course, being exposed to high playing time and long weekends is *not* detrimental to everyone, but it certainly doesn't help *most* players.

* * *

Battling with tough schedules, players must also be able to live comfortably. Teams do a fantastic job of accommodating room and board, utilities, and other variable expenses.

Like any profession, pay is extremely important. If you're not being paid, it's hard to make a living. If you're not making a living, it's a hard hill to overcome.

The ECHL, currently, does a pretty good job of teams paying their respective players, but with the cost of living steadily rising, it's on the edge of not being "enough."

According to the official ECHL website, these statistics based off of last year's numbers:

What is the salary cap in the ECHL?

The weekly salary cap for 2018-19 is $13,470 per week for the first 30 days of the season and $13,000 per week for the balance of the season. The weekly salary floor is $9,850.

What is the minimum salary for an ECHL player?

Teams are required in 2018-19 to pay rookie players a minimum salary of $470 per week and returning players a minimum salary of $510 per week. A returning player is classified as a player who appeared on a team's season-ending or playoff roster or who has played in 25 or more professional hockey games.

What is the NHL/AHL affiliate payment?

The NHL/AHL affiliate payment for 2018-19 is $525 per week. Any affiliate amount other than $525 per week agreed upon with any NHL/AHL club will be considered a salary cap violation. This includes excess payments for equipment, travel, etc.[67]

ECHL players receive room and board, as well as the amenities and facilities, equipment, paid leave for emergencies, and various insurances. If you're down from the AHL or NHL, you're paid that portion of salary. The ECHL team, in turn, pays the NHL/AHL affiliate payment of $525 per week—making it a great deal to have NHL or AHL-contracted players to be on the team.

---

67   "Frequently Asked Questions." 2019. Echl.Com.

But, in most cases, the money isn't completely there—even though the current collective bargaining agreement (CBA) in place for the ECHL is demonstrating pay increases yearly. Do the math, and you'll realize that it's not a whole lot that an ECHL player makes. While their living expenses are paid for when they're in hockey season, pay starts to dissipate as the season comes to a close. Many players have to supplement with summer jobs to be able to make ends' meet, and prepare for a future that is often blurry. Unless, of course, you're on an aforementioned NHL or AHL contract.

In the case of prospects on NHL contracts, they're living rather comfortably at the ECHL level, being on the NHL deal. However, if a player is unsigned by an NHL club and on an AHL/ECHL deal, the pay may not be there.

However, less pay is another added motivation needed to get to a higher level, per Jacob MacDonald. "I think one of the biggest lessons that I took away in East Coast League, was you know, you're not really playing for the money. Obviously, we're not making a lot. You're playing for the love of the game, and to continue to make yourself a better hockey player." The love of the game certainly fuels others as well, and it makes it so much more rewarding to move on to another league and have higher pay.

"I make sure I remember that I only made... $480 a week at one point in my hobby," MacDonald added. It's funny to have listened to him say it, but even funnier to read it. My hobbies sometimes *cost* me $480 in a week. Don't do game-worn jerseys, kids.

Colby Armstrong, a former NHL player and analyst in the present, whose brother Riley is the coach of the Maine Mariners, signed a contract with the ECHL's Utah Grizzlies during the 2012–13 lockout. He didn't play a game, but learned that players aren't playing for the money. In one instance, the team had to sign an EBUG—or emergency backup goaltender—to a contract. Because of the weekly salary cap restrictions, there had to be contract and salary negotiations in the locker room, before the game. In Armstrong's words, "I was thinking: this is hockey. Guys were saying 'okay, I'll take $100 less, I just want to play'."[68]

It's a speculation that with room and board and the weekly salary, players are typically "living" at around $3,000 to $4,000 (USD) per month in total value—including the living expenses, but *before taxes* which obviously vary on a state-to-state or provincial basis. It isn't too bad, but then the off-season hits, and those numbers wholly dissipate. Assuming that the player is on the team from October to April, and making around $2000 per month in take-home wages, $16,000 is *not* a lot of money to put away for the future or for living comfortably in the Summer.

---

68   Gordon, Sean. "Colby Armstrong On Life In The ECHL."
2013(updated 2018). The Globe And Mail.

During the off-season, players must make their own money, at that time.

While some players work part-time, others enroll in college in hopes of furthering their education. Some players even take classes during their season. As much as everyone hopes that hockey will be a steady financial outlet for the rest of their lives, that dream is often compromised and most players must find a way to compensate for that. An education gives them potential in another profession, instead of being completely reliant on one that can fade from within their lives as quickly as a puck misses the net.

For instance, Terrence Wallin of the Maine Mariners has recently started his own skill development camp, called Evolution Hockey; it's a way of teaching others, continuing his skills, and also maintaining a supplementary income during the off-season.

However, even with uncertainty about what a player makes or spends, it's up to the player on what they do with their extra funds. Riley Armstrong had this remark about the money management side of things: "We pay for all the bills that a player gets throughout the course of the year with his apartment. And we pay for his rent as well... So when you're getting that, say you're getting 900 bucks every two weeks and you don't have any bills, I think that's up to the player on what they want to do. I don't know if they like shoes or they like to go check out the movies every night, but I think there is a time where those players can save a little bit of money." This is entirely true, but even so, $1,800 for a month of playing isn't the perfect scenario.

Of course, you have to take more than just the players into perspective. You have to look at the league as a whole. It's not the NHL. You don't have 18,000 people showing up per game. You may have 2,400 one game, and 3,200 the next. If attendance numbers were bigger across the board in the ECHL, pay would be too. The ECHL and PHPA do a good job of making sure players are paid, but it could still be better.

The ECHL, though they do offer competitive pay, with each passing year, the cost of living goes up and so should their salary cap. Of course, this is much easier said than done.

Also, the ECHL is not the only league that competes to sign players. Various other leagues internationally sign free agents frequently, and are often willing to give the same pay if not more than what ECHL teams offer them. The moral dilemma for players is: Will this hurt or help my chances at the NHL?

It's incredibly difficult to gage whether or not a move to another league is more beneficial than playing in the ECHL for their development, but if the pay is there, it may be the deciding factor in the comparison of competing leagues.

CHAPTER 15

STREAMLINING DEVELOPMENT

———

Few teams are willing to show the same level of interest and dedication to prospect development as the Newfoundland Growlers. It starts at the top, and is a trickle-down effect into the minor league ranks. The trickle-down effect eventually does stop, at the Southern Professional Hockey League level, as players from the SPHL are typically signed to PTO's on ECHL teams. The SPHL does not have an affiliation with any ECHL teams, either.

One of the largest problems at the moment is that not every NHL and AHL team have an ECHL affiliation that is strictly to their organization. There are twenty-six current ECHL teams, as opposed to thirty-one AHL teams and thirty-one

NHL teams. This essentially means that farm systems are not completely developed and aligned, and players that play less minutes at the AHL level, or players that are not ready for the AHL level, are not able to go elsewhere to develop.

As of the 2019-20 season, here are the current affiliations:

ECHL Team	AHL Affiliate	NHL Affiliate
Adirondack Thunder	Binghamton Devils	New Jersey Devils
Allen Americans	Iowa Wild	Minnesota Wild
Atlanta Gladiators	Providence Bruins	Boston Bruins
Brampton Beast	Belleville Senators	Ottawa Senators
Cincinnati Cyclones	Rochester Americans	Buffalo Sabres
Florida Everblades	Milwaukee Admirals	Nashville Predators
Fort Wayne Komets	Chicago Wolves	Vegas Golden Knights
Greenville Swamp Rabbits	Charlotte Checkers	Carolina Hurricanes
Idaho Steelheads	Texas Stars	Dallas Stars
Indy Fuel	Rockford IceHogs	Chicago Blackhawks
Jacksonville Icemen	Manitoba Moose	Winnipeg Jets
Kalamazoo Wings	Utica Comets	Vancouver Canucks
Kansas City Mavericks	Stockton Heat	Calgary Flames
Maine Mariners	Hartford Wolf Pack	New York Rangers
Newfoundland Growlers	Toronto Marlies	Toronto Maple Leafs
Norfolk Admirals	*Independent*	*Independent*
Orlando Solar Bears	Syracuse Crunch	Tampa Bay Lightning
Rapid City Rush	Tucson Roadrunners	Arizona Coyotes
Reading Royals	Lehigh Valley Phantoms	Philadelphia Flyers
South Carolina Stingrays	Hershey Bears	Washington Capitals
Toledo Walleye	Grand Rapids Griffins	Detroit Red Wings
Tulsa Oilers	San Antonio Rampage	St. Louis Blues
Utah Grizzlies	Colorado Eagles	Colorado Avalanche
Wheeling Nailers	Wilkes-Barre/Scranton Penguins	Pittsburgh Penguins
Wichita Thunder	Bakersfield Condors	Edmonton Oilers
Worcester Railers	Bridgeport Sound Tigers	New York Islanders

69

---

69 "NHL/AHL Affiliations.". 2019. Echl.Com.

The Montréal Canadiens, Los Angeles Kings, Anaheim Ducks, Columbus Blue Jackets, San Jose Sharks, and Florida Panthers systems all lack an official ECHL affiliation. *This is a problem.* In an ideal world, there should be a 31/31/31 spread, to streamline all prospect development. As a result of this, players that do not make AHL squads for these clubs often find themselves in different systems with different personnel that may not be ideal for the AHL/NHL squads that they do belong to.

Though there are twenty-six ECHL teams, it is important to note that the Norfolk Admirals have no AHL or ECHL affiliation—which is an oversight by NHL teams, though I wouldn't be surprised to see something in the works for next season. It seems that many teams are neutral as to what they'd like to do with their ECHL teams, some teams don't particularly utilize them, and other teams utilize them as important developmental pieces.

This can especially be seen by teams that limit their roster moves with the AHL, essentially creating a stagnant lineup for the year that does not contribute to upper levels; in teams that work closely with the NHL, or at the request of the NHL and AHL teams, they may manage the ECHL lineup, including what prospects see more time than others.

There's reasoning behind the little moves, though. The Cincinnati Cyclones only used twenty-nine players this past year.[70] Four of those players are goalies. Very little turnover via transactions, means that everyone is playing with each other, gaining team chemistry, and creating a great product on the ice—as the Cyclones ended up first in the league at the end of the regular season. Basically, they were built to be an ECHL powerhouse, which they were.

But they weren't churning out players to the AHL in their Rochester affiliate, and despite the point totals of many of the players on the team, most are veteran ECHL guys that are seemingly past that initial prospect development phase. Looking at the Cyclones' streamline of affiliations, with Rochester and Buffalo, it seems that Buffalo isn't particularly interested in having more young players that are succeeding at the ECHL level up to their AHL affiliate. Which is, kind of weird.

In fact, a prime example of this on Cincinnati's roster is Russian-born center Vasili Glotov, who, despite having fifty points in sixty-eight games this season, at the youthful age of twenty-one, only played two games in the AHL.[71]

Meanwhile, a team like the Maine Mariners, affiliated with the Wolf Pack and thusly the Rangers, used fifty-seven players this year. FIFTY-SEVEN. There were transactions happening

---

70 "Elite Prospects - 2018-19 Cincinnati Cyclones." Elite Prospects, 2019.
71 "Elite Prospects - Vasili Glotov." Elite Prospects, 2019.

at a rate of what seemed to be at least twice a week between various AHL teams (because of "unofficial" ties with Laval). Many players had extended call-ups, or were sent down, then developed and were called back up.

Working with Chris Drury of the Wolf Pack, there were many players that had opportunities to develop at the AHL level. Riley Armstrong made sure to note that, "Pat Boller comes to games, the assistant GM for Hartford; he's at games all the time. They're always watching. I'm sending reports to them about players here."

With the contingent of Montréal's affiliate, the Laval Rocket, there were also a number of players that had played for the Mariners throughout the season given an opportunity to succeed at the AHL level in Laval as opposed to Hartford. Players like fan favorites Morgan Adams-Moisan, Connor LaCouvee, and Alex Kile played considerable amounts of time in Laval, though Adams-Moisan had started the season as the only of Laval's property of the three names.

With how the game is trending, it's possible that several years from now, we could see an NHL-AHL-ECHL linear development model become the standard for professional hockey in North America.

Armstrong laid out to me what we mutually agree will most likely see happen:

"This could be run like baseball - where you can maybe sign a three way contract for NHL money, AHL money, and ECHL money... I think the way that you see the NHL going with these bigger contracts (Marner, Mattthews, McDavid, etc.)... where are all these young guys going to go every two to three years?"

A player can only stay in the junior or college ranks for so long. And once they're at the AHL rank—if they're not getting playing time and there isn't an ECHL team in the organization, what happens?

"I think their [NHL teams'] pools are going to get so big. I think teams are going to be forced to buy an ECHL team where they're going to be developing players coming up all the time."

It's going to be the streamlined developmental model. The only problem with this is fielding those additional ECHL teams in such a short period of time, especially with Seattle becoming another NHL team in the near future. While one would hope that a linear developmental model would be this close to fruition, five years may be a bit more optimistic than tangible of a timeline.

CHAPTER 16

PARTIALLY ELIMINATING THE BASH AND CRASH STYLE

———

It's certainly not what the casual hockey fan wants. If you ever played *NHL Hitz 2002* on an older generation video game console like the PlayStation 2, you grew up to love that style of play, even if it were ridiculous, and oftentimes cheesy.

For the ECHL, the bash and crash style is the brick-and-mortar style of play for the league. Part of the foundation of the league was built on this style.

This style of play would be incredibly hard to eliminate completely, but with the way that the game is going and growing with more emphasis on speed and finesse, rather than a rough and tumble style of play, it may be something that can eventually be reached.

What I'm not saying is take out fighting, take out hitting, and making it a noncontact sport. I don't want to see the transition that Maine boys' high school hockey has gone through.

I say "partially eliminating," because there is too much fighting and too many penalties at this time within the league.

For reference, there were forty-nine players in the 2018–19 ECHL regular season that had over one hundred penalty minutes, and of those forty-nine players, ten had over 200 penalty minutes.[72] For the AHL regular season, there were just twenty-eight players over one hundred penalty minutes, with the highest amount being 154 penalty minutes.[73] For the NHL regular season, as one can probably imagine, those numbers took even more of a decline. Just six players had over one hundred penalty minutes.[74]

It is evident that at the highest league in the world, that bash and crash style is almost gone. Only ten years ago in the

72 "Elite Prospects - ECHL PIM Stats 2018-2019." Elite Prospects, 2019.
73 "Elite Prospects - AHL PIM Stats 2018-19." Elite Prospects, 2019.
74 "Elite Prospects - NHL PIM Stats 2018-19." Elite Prospects, 2019.

2008–09 season, there were sixty players that had over one hundred penalty minutes in regular season NHL games.[75]

Sixty players, and now down to six. The style that many loved is truly fading away.

Of course, this isn't to say that those forty-nine ECHL players are all "goons" or "Doug Glatt's" of the world—even with some players hitting over 200 penalty minutes. Of the ten players hitting over 200 penalty minutes, four players put up thirty plus points. Of the remaining thirty-nine, several players hit fifty to sixty and close to seventy points, with a bunch of players hitting thirty to forty points.[76]

Sure, there is someone like Yannick Turcotte, who scored two goals and added three assists, as well as 186 penalty minutes, in just forty-two games, but those enforcer-esque players are now few and far between.[77]

However, I'm all for keeping grinders. And, I know I'm not alone.

"The crash bang, the grind, that playoff style of hockey that you saw with the St Louis Blues. I think that's always going to

75 "Elite Prospects - NHL PIM Stats 2008-09." Elite Prospects, 2019.
76 "Elite Prospects - ECHL PIM Stats 2018-2019." Elite Prospects, 2019.
77 "Elite Prospects - Yannick Turcotte." Elite Prospects, 2019.

be part of the game," Mariners coach Riley Armstrong said. But, there are some parts of the game that simply are not part of the game anymore. Enforcers, truthfully, are one of those roles that doesn't fit in with how the game is moving. If you're a fan of them, enjoy the true "Last of The Enforcers" with a player like Turcotte. "I think fighting's just slowly going to go out and it's more of a respect factor that players are respecting each other a little more. With the amount of awareness that has been brought to the forefront with concussions, you don't see a lot of guys taking vicious runs at guys to hurt them and things like that."

I asked him where he sees this league from a physical stand-point in five years: "I feel, like I said, the hitting is going to be there. But, I don't think there will be any fighting in five years." A player like Turcotte really is one of the last of a dying breed.

I can understand Knappe's concerns back in Chapter 13 about dropping a young player (i.e., Semyon Der-Arguchintsev) into a league like this—though I still think it ultimately ben-efits them.

One of the major concerns in dropping players like Der-Argu-chintsev into this league, though, is that there is not enough discipline of players, nor are there enough disciplinary reper-cussions to players who engage in this style of play.

I think that the best bet in resolving this issue is to develop stricter disciplinary measures, including the likes of match penalties and suspensions. As of right now, both of these seem to be incredibly inconsistent amongst referees. Of course, this is to be expected, given the fact that referees, like players, are trying to progress to the next level and inconsistencies are expected given that a league will always have "good" refs and "bad" refs.

The senseless violence that often results in concussions and potentially career-jeopardizing injuries, though, need to come to a complete halt.

The ECHL does indeed market itself in one way or another based on the bash and crash style. To eliminate that will result in the loss of some fans, but it is inevitable that the league is going to move past that style into more of a modern style.

The transition is in the works, and it's almost complete.

The enforcer died. The bash and crash style is being phased out. There will still be instances of it inherent in the game, like what was seen in the St. Louis Blues' Stanley Cup run. But, it'll be something rare to see in the near future.

CHAPTER 17

PLAYERS TO LOOK OUT FOR IN THE 2019–20 ECHL SEASON

To cap off this book, let's take a look at twenty-six players for all twenty-six teams that should be worth keeping an eye on for this 2019–20 ECHL season. All of them are slated to start the year at this level:

Adirondack Thunder

Michael McNiven (G)—Signed by the Montréal Canadiens, McNiven is part of the Canadiens' goaltending circus. Cayden Primeau and Charlie Lindgren are starting the year in the AHL, sending McNiven to Adirondack and LaCouvee to Maine.

Primeau is expected to stay at the AHL level the entire year, but with Lindgren's job in jeopardy with more goaltending talent waiting in the wings in the ECHL, expect this year to be a statement year for McNiven as he battles for a return to AHL action.

Allen Americans

Gabriel Gagné (RW)—A rangy winger, Gagné has had a hard time transitioning from major junior to the professional ranks. In 2015, the Ottawa Senators traded up and drafted him in round two, number thirty-six overall. By the 2017–18 season, things seemed to be trending up for him statistically, posting twenty goals and adding five assists in his second season of AHL action. But, after a disappointing 2018–19 season that saw him score just nine points in thirty-three AHL games, he became an unrestricted free agent and signed with Allen. While he hasn't lived up to expectations, he's still just twenty-two, and this season could be the season to really turn things around for him.[78]

Atlanta Gladiators

Dante Hannoun (C)—The opposite size of Gagné, Hannoun is just 5'6 at twenty-one years of age. Following a solid junior career in the WHL with Prince Albert and Victoria in which he

---

78 "Elite Prospects - Gabriel Gagné." Elite Prospects, 2019.

averaged 0.89 points per game in the regular season, it will be interesting to see how the diminutive centerman adjusts to the professional play. With his small stature and the game trending toward more of a finesse game, perhaps Hannoun can take advantage of this transition despite the barrier that is his size. He's a player not to miss, but you may miss him, given his size.[79]

Brampton Beast

<u>François Beauchemin (RW)</u>—This is not the same François Beauchemin who played so many years of NHL action. This Beauchemin is twenty-three years old, and split time between Belleville of the AHL and Brampton last year. However, it seemed that he regressed from his first year in the AHL to his second last year, though he puts up consistent point totals in the ECHL.[80] Like many players, he'll be working hard to get back on an AHL roster.

Cincinnati Cyclones

<u>Jesse Schultz (RW)</u>—The oldest player on this list at the ripe age of thirty-seven years, it's clear that Schultz's career is most likely not going to progress into the AHL, but he still remains one of the best players to watch for in the ECHL. He's worked

---

79 "Elite Prospects - Dante Hannoun." Elite Prospects, 2019.
80 "Elite Prospects - François Beauchemin." Elite Prospects, 2019.

for every bit of his success at this level, and is poised to be another leader on a potent and dangerous offense again this year for the Cyclones. Schultz has made a name for himself as an elite ECHL playmaker, posting fifty-eight and fifty-seven assist campaigns in his last two years, respectively.[81]

Florida Everblades

<u>Ken Appleby (G)</u>—Appleby had the rare feat of playing in the ECHL, AHL, and NHL in the 2017-18 season. However, in the 2018-19 season, he was relegated to ECHL and AHL action only. While his numbers at the ECHL level were sparkling, his AHL numbers—a 3.92 GAA and .884 SV% over ten games—were not.[82] It's clear that Appleby can perform at the ECHL level, but hasn't been his best at the AHL level as of late. Like McNiven, this year is going to be an effort to turn things around and get back to goaltending at the AHL level.

Fort Wayne Komets

<u>Alan Lyszczarczyk (C)</u>—Lyszczarczyk is another of the twenty-one-year-olds coming from the CHL, off of the OHL's Mississauga Steelheads. After starting the season with eleven points in ten games for Owen Sound,

---

81 "Elite Prospects - Jesse Schultz." Elite Prospects, 2019.
82 "Elite Prospects - Ken Appleby." Elite Prospects, 2019.

Lyszczarczyk put up career highs in goals (thirty-five) and assists (thirty-six) in the regular season. He's also got plenty of international experience, playing for the Polish men's national team each of the past two years and the U20 junior team twice.[83] While neither of the teams are in the respective highest divisions of international play, he's been consistent with his production and could use the ECHL as his place to breakout and shine.

Greenville Swamp Rabbits

Patrick Bajkov (RW/LW)—Though property of the Florida Panthers, Bajkov will start the year playing in the ECHL for Greenville, who is affiliated with Charlotte and Carolina, because the Panthers do not have an ECHL affiliate. Bajkov, age twenty-one, has a knack for producing offensively as seen by his one hundred point season in 2017-18 with the Everett Silvertips of the WHL. However, he struggled in his first year professionally finding any sort of offensive prowess, scoring just four goals and adding fourteen assists in thirty-three games between Manchester and Florida in the ECHL last season. He did manage three goals and two assists at the AHL level.[84] Expect this year to be a fine sophomore season for the young winger.

---

83 "Elite Prospects - Alan Lyszczarczyk." Elite Prospects, 2019.
84 "Elite Prospects - Patrick Bajkov." Elite Prospects, 2019.

Idaho Steelheads

Colton Point (G)—Point had a phenomenal last year of college hockey in the 2017-18 season with NCAA Division I Colgate University. He had an incredible 1.74 GAA and .944 SV% over thirty-three games. He was even selected to play for Team Canada at the 2018 World Junior Hockey Championship, appearing in one game and allowing zero goals. The Dallas Stars' signed goaltender had a rude awakening to the professional level, though. He posted an abysmal 3.77 GAA and .857 SV% in seven AHL games, and a marginally better 3.28 GAA and .887 SV% in thirteen ECHL games.[85] This is by no means the end of the line for such a young goaltender with so much potential, but things need to turn around for the better.

Indy Fuel

Keoni Texeira (D)—Texeira was ranked #143 by NHL Central Scouting in his 2015 NHL draft year, but wasn't selected. The former Portland Winterhawks defenseman had a modest WHL career from an offensive perspective. However, after signing with the Wichita Thunder last year, Texeira exploded for forty-six points in seventy games in his first full professional season.[86] While he had a chance to crack the AHL's

---

85   "Elite Prospects - Colton Point." Elite Prospects, 2019.
86   "Elite Prospects - Keoni Texeira." Elite Prospects, 2019.

Rockford IceHogs to begin the season, he's going to start the year in Indy, but I wouldn't be surprised if Rockford or another AHL team took notice with impressive numbers like that as a defenseman.

Jacksonville IceMen

Alexis D'Aoust (RW)—The French-Canadian winger had no trouble finding the scoresheet at the ECHL level last year, generating seven goals and fifteen points in just eleven contests. At nearly 100 games of AHL experience, it's surprising that he gets the start for this season in the ECHL, but I don't reckon he'll be down for long.[87] If he's able to replicate his success, he should be back up at the AHL level in no time. Of course, Jacksonville is a long way from Manitoba, so hopefully it's a one way flight.

Kalamazoo Wings

Dylan Sadowy (LW/RW)—Sadowy, a former San Jose Sharks third round draft pick, was over a point per game at the ECHL level in the regular season last year, but like prior years, has struggled at the AHL level mightily. Sadowy managed just one goal in fourteen AHL games last year.[88] He's still relatively

---

87 "Elite Prospects - Alexis D'Aoust." Elite Prospects, 2019.
88 "Elite Prospects - Dylan Sadowy." Elite Prospects, 2019.

young at just twenty-three, but the time for him to progress with a strong showing in the ECHL and back to the AHL is now. He's proven himself at the ECHL level and played a bunch of games at the AHL level, but the production just hasn't been there. Expect more of the same production-wise in the ECHL this year, but his potential to produce at a higher level is questionable.

Kansas City Mavericks

Hayden Hawkey (G)—With his last name, nothing else should matter. You have to root for a guy with a name like this. And considering he's fresh out of cawlidge hawkey, it's like a fairytale. He's twenty-four years of age, which is a little bit on the later side to turn pro, but his numbers were brilliant with NCAA Division I Providence last year. Forty-one games, a 1.88 GAA and .921 SV%.[89] Again, there's no way that you can't root for this guy. And given his track record of success, he *should* have a solid first professional year.

Maine Mariners

Ty Ronning (RW)—He's a great player on the ice, and a great person off the ice. Maybe he gets some of it from his dad, Cliff. Ronning had sixty-one goals in seventy games in his last year in the WHL in 2017-18, and while he wasn't particularly

---

89 "Elite Prospects - Hayden Hawkey." Elite Prospects, 2019.

productive at the AHL level this past year with four goals and one assist in twenty-three games, he scored twelve goals and added ten assists in twenty-five ECHL games.[90] In fact, in his first ECHL game, he had three goals and two assists resulting in a comeback win. He had flashes of brilliance. He's got the raw talent, but there are other parts of his game that still need work. Realistically, expect a monster ECHL season from this guy, regardless of however long he stays down—meaning, he won't be down here the entire season. His one downfall is that he seemingly struggles staying healthy with injury problems.

Newfoundland Growlers

<u>Giorgio Estephan (C)</u>—Estephan, mentioned earlier in the book, had an impressive 2018-19 season with Newfoundland, and was one of the key cogs in their Kelly Cup run and win. He had fifty-three points in sixty-nine games in the regular season, but really came alive during the playoffs with twenty-four points in twenty-three games.[91] He's becoming more and more of a well-rounded player, and should be seeing more AHL time in the near future. He's got the offense down—now it's more about bringing it all together. The Canadian centerman is sure to be another key piece in what looks to be another title-contending Newfoundland Growlers roster.

---

90 "Elite Prospects - Ty Ronning." Elite Prospects, 2019.
91 "Elite Prospects - Giorgio Estephan." Elite Prospects, 2019.

Norfolk Admirals

Brandon Halverson (G)—Halverson was the Maine Mariners' starting goaltender for much of last year, and even showed up on the SportsCenter Top 10 one night after a miraculous goal-line stop. He played a good amount of games in Hartford as well. In a contract year, 'Halvy' was not offered a new contract by the team that had drafted him, the New York Rangers. He was on a try-out with the Toronto Maple Leafs, sent down to the Toronto Marlies training camp, sent down to the New-foundland Growlers training camp and subsequently released from his PTO, eventually finding his way into Norfolk. For a team that has no AHL or NHL affiliation, this may be the best move for Halverson as it gives him the potential to be looked at by a variety of organizations. Of course, this is if he plays to his highest ability. He'll surely be in constant competition with Anaheim Ducks goaltending prospect, Roman Durný, though.

Orlando Solar Bears

Zach Fucale/Zach Sawchenko/Spencer Martin (G)—It was impossible to pick one of the three goaltenders. All three goaltenders were very highly-touted goaltenders in their respective draft classes. However, Sawchenko was not selected, which came as a surprise to many. Given his success at the U Sports level the past two years, it's still rather surprising. Fucale, on the other hand, was a second round pick in 2013 by the Montréal

Canadiens, and has fallen well short of expectations to this point. And to make things crazier, Spencer Martin has played three NHL games, and is on contract with the Tampa Bay Lightning. It's the ECHL's version of a three-headed goaltending monster, and it'll be interesting to see how this all plays out.

Rapid City Rush

Keeghan Howdeshell (LW)—Howdeshell led the Sault Ste. Marie Greyhounds of the OHL in goals last year with forty-six in sixty-six games.[92] However, it is important to note that playing with an elite NHL prospect like Morgan Frost is quite beneficial. Still, forty-six goals in the OHL is a talking point, and the winger is poised to take on a scoring role for a Rapid City team that came in last in goals for last season with just 168 in seventy-two games.[93] Given good company, he could put up impressive totals in his first professional season—especially if Rapid City still has a hard time scoring.

Reading Royals

Kirill Ustimenko (G)—Ustimenko, a goaltender on contract with the Philadelphia Flyers, will be battling Felix Sandstrom, another goaltender on contract with the Philadelphia Flyers.

---

92 "Elite Prospects - Keeghan Howdeshell." Elite Prospects, 2019.
93 "2018-19 Regular Season Standings." Echl.Com. 2019.

Sandstrom played most of his games last year in the SHL, whilst Ustimenko played a season in the MHL, which is essentially Russia's major junior league. I give the edge to Ustimenko as more of a player to watch, though, as he's only twenty while Sandstrom is twenty-two. Reading didn't have much in the way of NHL prospects last year, but this year is going to be different. Ustimenko's MHL numbers are a sign of great things to come, with a 1.78 GAA and .927 SV% over forty-six games.[94] Starting in the ECHL will be a great way to transition to the North American game, and potentially the same workload.

South Carolina Stingrays

Cameron Askew (C/RW)—The former QMJHL veteran of 327 games will be entering his second season in the ECHL, looking to improve upon a respectable seventeen goals and ten assists through forty-seven regular season contests last year.[95] At age twenty-two, Askew is one of the youngest members of the Stingrays, but is carrying over so much experience from major junior that the transition has been much easier for the professional game. He's a bit of a wild-card with what his production could look like this coming season.

---

94 "Elite Prospects - Kirill Ustimenko." Elite Prospects, 2019.
95 "Elite Prospects - Cameron Askew." Elite Prospects, 2019.

Toledo Walleye

Charle-Edouard D'Astous (D)—Another QMJHL alum, D'Astous was the captain of the Rimouski Océanic last year, and had strong offensive outputs with sixty-six points in fifty-five games—an incredible feat for a defenseman to be over a point per game. Having leadership experience and offensive potential is a great combination for a twenty-one year old. At 6'2, he has some size too.[96] If things go as planned, the youthful D'Astous could be a steal for a team that has the highest average age in the entire league to start the season.[97]

Tulsa Oilers

Robby Jackson (C)—A relatively small centerman at just 5'9, Jackson is coming off a great final year at NCAA Division I St. Cloud State, posting forty points in thirty-seven games. Having just turned twenty-two years of age in August, Jackson is in a good position to make strides for Tulsa. He played in three games in the AHL last year, scoring his first professional goal, and should have a bevy of good wingers to work with.[98]

96 "Elite Prospects - Charle-Edouard D'Astous." Elite Prospects, 2019.
97 "Elite Prospects - 2019-20 Toledo Walleye." Elite Prospects, 2019.
98 "Elite Prospects - Robby Jackson." Elite Prospects, 2019.

Utah Grizzlies

<u>Travis Barron (LW)</u>—Barron just turned twenty-one years of age in August, and is on contract with the Colorado Avalanche. Barron split time between the ECHL and AHL last year. He played in thirty-eight AHL games but only managed three goals and two assists. Playing in twelve ECHL games, he had two goals and six assists.[99] With a full season under his belt, Barron should see an uptick in performance this upcoming year after finding his bearings. Like other players to watch out for this season, it wouldn't be too much of a surprise if he was called up to the AHL sooner rather than later, especially with the Avalanche playing a hand in his development. As an added storyline, his cousin, Cole Cassels, is also on the Utah Grizzlies this year, ironically coming from Grizzlys Wolfsburg of the DEL.[100] Perhaps some sort of family chemistry is in store.

Wheeling Nailers

<u>Jan Drozg (LW)</u>—At just twenty years of age, Drozg is one of the younger players in the ECHL, and on the first year of his entry-level deal with the Pittsburgh Penguins. The speedy Slovenian winger is best known for his offensive capabilities, and likely part of why he's starting the year in the

---

99 "Elite Prospects - Travis Barron." Elite Prospects, 2019.
100 "Elite Prospects - Cole Cassels." Elite Prospects, 2019.

ECHL—to better his defensive capabilities. He had a stagger-
ingly ugly minus thirty-five plus/minus rating last year in the
QMJHL,[101] but to be fair, his team only managed fourteen
wins the entire year.[102] He led the team in scoring with six-
ty-two points in sixty games,[103] and was somewhat of a bright
light in an otherwise dark and depressing season otherwise.

Wichita Thunder

Dylan Wells (G)—Wells is in the second year of his entry-
level deal with the Edmonton Oilers, and at age twenty-one,
should be the starter for Wichita this season. However, Mitch
Gillam will be giving it his all too. Wells is in an odd position in the Edmonton Oilers organization, though. Shane
Starrett is in his final year of his contract, and put up great
AHL numbers last year in Bakersfield. Stuart Skinner, also
in the second year of his entry-level deal with the Oilers, is
currently in the AHL over Wells, with Starrett. With Olivier
Rodrigue in the pipeline in the QMJHL but signed and most
likely turning pro at the end of this year, Wells will have to
battle hard to get back to the AHL level this season, which
could potentially result in a great goaltending battle between
Skinner, Starrett and Wells.

---

101 "Elite Prospects - Jan Drozg." Elite Prospects, 2019.
102 "Elite Prospects - 2018-19 Shawinigan Cataractes." Elite
     Prospects, 2019.
103 "Elite Prospects - Jan Drozg." Elite Prospects, 2019.

Worcester Railers

<u>Jakub Skarek (G)</u>—At just nineteen years of age, Skarek will be amongst the very youngest players in the league to start the season, though he does turn twenty a month into the season. As a signed prospect of the New York Islanders, Skarek will be transitioning to the North American game much like Kirill Ustimenko of Reading. Skarek played twenty-two games in Liiga last year, posting a modest 2.45 GAA and .906 SV% in Finland's top league.[104] Let me reiterate: he's nineteen. Skarek is ahead of schedule, so-to-speak.

---

104 "Elite Prospects - Jakub Skarek." Elite Prospects, 2019.

FINAL THOUGHTS

Through hard work, perseverance, and a dedication to not only hockey, but all facets of being a professional athlete, 662 former ECHL alumni have reached the NHL as of the end of the 2018-19 season. There is no denying, with that many alumni, that the ECHL is a true developmental league for NHL-caliber players. That, the ECHL, is a breeding ground for future NHL talent.

It is by no means an easy road, and most of the time, does not happen in the course of one season.

It is defined by the word "grind."

While the ECHL is making progress in the right direction with player development, there is still a lot of work that needs to be done to make this league into a fully-fledged develop-mental hockey league, including the utilization of all NHL teams—not just some.

There has to be a superior element of trust from the NHL, down to the AHL, and finally the ECHL, that players will be safe, will be able to live comfortably, be given access to ame-nities and facilities, and will play and train to be professional players both on and off the ice.

While I believe that this has been mutually achieved by some organizations—highlighted by Readinga, Maine and New-foundland and their respective parent clubs, it hasn't spread through the entire league just yet.

While I have no doubt that the ECHL is completely able and willing to make this their future, I am unsure of the timeline in which they are able to do that, as teams can't magically be created like they are in an *EA Sports NHL Franchise* video game mode.

As it stands currently, only having twenty-six ECHL teams, and twenty-five of them affiliated with thirty-one NHL teams, is a problem. Another problem will be encountered when the thirty-second team in Seattle comes into play in the NHL.

The ECHL needs an expansion. Though they did drop the "East Coast Hockey League" tagline in 2003, the majority of teams are still on the East Coast, which makes it hard for teams like Los Angeles, San Jose, and Anaheim—the California trifecta—to utilize them; more ECHL teams must be added to the western United States, or Canada. Los Angeles has their AHL team close by in Ontario, San Jose has their AHL team close by in San Jose, and Anaheim follows suit with their AHL team in San Diego. Manchester just folded in the Los Angeles system, but it was not exactly ideal to have them on the polar opposite side of the country, which was a big reason why the Monarchs as an AHL team were moved to Ontario, California, to begin with.

Manchester is obviously a candidate for another ECHL team, though the city is unfortunately a very hard sell on tickets, currently.

I think that there are also other potential locations for ECHL hockey on both sides of North America—it's just whether or not it will be financially viable for not only the league and organizations, but the cities too.

As the 2019–20 season rolls around, I wish nothing but the best for all of the players that I've talked to, as well as management, and fans.

If you want to talk hockey, or maybe have me sign this book (a man can hope, right?), feel free to swing on by to a Maine

Mariners game. Section V, row 15, dead center. I'm usually in my LaCouvee Wild Blueberries jersey, or my Ronning Nickelodeon jersey. You can't miss me. I'm usually one of the tallest people there.

I believe that my Mariners will be much better this season than the last—given that we pretty much dropped a goose egg the final ten games of the season. We've signed a few of our key guys back, and got some NHL-caliber goaltenders and prospects from New York and Hartford to start the year.

I hope you've enjoyed the book. Thank you for your support of the ECHL, AHL, NHL, PHPA, and the sport of ice hockey, in general.

...

Go Mariners!

APPENDIX

CHAPTER 1: EVERY PLAYER HAS THEIR STORY

"Alex Burrows Was The Unlikeliest Success Story In Canucks History." 2017. Vancouver Courier.

"ECHL Alumni." 2019. echl.com. Accessed July 9, 2019.

"Elite Prospects - ECHL PIM Stats 2018-2019." Elite Prospects, 2019.

CHAPTER 2: THE THING ABOUT PROSPECT DEVELOPMENT

Grainda, Mark. 2018. "Why A Former ECHL Forward Headed Overseas." The Sin Bin.

McKenna, Mike. 2010. "How Do The NHL, AHL And ECHL Differ - A Goalie's Perspective." InGoal Magazine.

CHAPTER 3: A BRIEF HISTORY OF THE EAST COAST HOCKEY LEAGUE

"ECHL History." 2019. Echl.Com.

Elliott, Helene. 1998. "Goaltender Mclennan's Biggest Save Was His Life." Los Angeles Times.

CHAPTER 4: SHANE HARPER

"Elite Prospects - Shane Harper." Elite Prospects, 2019.

McKenna, Mike. 'PHPA Annual Meeting.' Instagram. June 28, 2016.

"Man Of The Year Team Award Winners Named." 2016. Theahl.Com.

Staff Writer. "Florida Panthers Re-Sign Forward Shane Harper". 2016. NHL.Com.

Staff Writer. "Future Watch: Shane Harper". 2012. NHL.Com.

CHAPTER 5: CONNOR LACOUVEE

"Elite Prospects - Connor LaCouvee." Elite Prospects, 2019.

MacMillan, Ken. 2019. "Montreal Canadiens Re-Sign Connor Lacouvee". A Winning Habit.

CHAPTER 6: JACOB MACDONALD

"Elite Prospects - 2014-15 Cornell University" Elite Prospects, 2019.

"Elite Prospects - Jacob MacDonald." Elite Prospects, 2019.

Golub, Sam. 2019. "Florida Panthers: Jacob Macdonald Deserves An NHL Role". The Rat Trick.

MacDonald, Jacob. 'Traded to Avalanche." Instagram. June 29, 2019.

CHAPTER 7: JOSH CURRIE

"Anaheim Ducks At Edmonton Oilers Box Score — February 23, 2019". 2019. Hockey-Reference.Com.

"CONDORS SIGN CURRIE AND O'BRIEN". 2017. Bakersfieldcondors.Com.

"Currie Signs AHL Contract". 2016. Bakersfieldcondors.Com.

"Elite Prospects - Josh Currie." Elite Prospects, 2019.

"Kremyr, Currie, And Little Agree To Terms". 2014. Bakersfieldcondors.Com.

CHAPTER 8: SEAN DAY

Cox, Damien. 2016. "Steelheads' Day Opens Up About Life Off The Ice." Sportsnet.Ca.

"Elite Prospects - Sean Day." Elite Prospects, 2019.

Joe, Curtis. 2015. "Elite Prospects - Sean Day." Elite Prospects.

CHAPTER 9: INCREASED PLAYING TIME → INCREASED OPPORTUNITIES

Allred Jr., Mark. 2019. "NHL Free Agency: Bruins To Sign Goaltender For Minor-Pro Depth". BLACK N GOLD HOCKEY PODCAST.

CHAPTER 10: PHYSICAL AND MENTAL PREPAREDNESS

"Elite Prospects - Ed Minney." Elite Prospects, 2019.

Monnich, Ted. 2016. "Monnich's Mental Game: Turning Goaltending Failure Into Success." Ingoal Magazine.

CHAPTER 11: THE IMPORTANCE OF EXPERIENCE AND CONNECTIONS

"Elite Prospects - Terrence Wallin." Elite Prospects, 2019.

"Elite Prospects - Zach Tolkinen." Elite Prospects, 2019.

CHAPTER 12: A MODEL DEVELOPMENTAL TEAM—THE NEWFOUNDLAND GROWLERS

Short, Robin. 2019. "A Good Start As A Starting Point: Newfoundland Growlers Doing 'A Great Job,' Says Maple Leafs' GM Kyle Dubas." Thetelegram.Com.

Staff Writer. "Ryane Clowe Named Head Coach Of Newfoundland Growlers." 2018. NHL.Com.

CHAPTER 13: THE STAGNANT NUMBERS

"About The PHPA." 2019. Phpa.Com.

"Elite Prospects - 2018-19 Newfoundland Growlers." Elite Prospects, 2019.

Knappe, Katya. 2019. "Have Kyle Dubas And The Leafs Turned The ECHL Into A Development League For NHL Players?" Pension Plan Puppets.

CHAPTER 14: BETTER SCHEDULING AND FINANCIAL STABILITY

"Frequently Asked Questions." 2019. Echl.Com.

Gordon, Sean. "Colby Armstrong On Life In The ECHL." 2013(updated 2018). The Globe And Mail.

CHAPTER 15: STREAMLINING DEVELOPMENT

"Elite Prospects - 2018-19 Cincinnati Cyclones." Elite Prospects, 2019.

"Elite Prospects - Vasili Glotov." Elite Prospects, 2019.

"NHL/AHL Affiliations.". 2019. Echl.Com.

CHAPTER 16: PARTIALLY ELIMINATING THE BASH AND CRASH STYLE

"Elite Prospects - AHL PIM Stats 2018-19." Elite Prospects, 2019.

"Elite Prospects - ECHL PIM Stats 2018-2019." Elite Prospects, 2019.

"Elite Prospects - NHL PIM Stats 2018-19." Elite Prospects, 2019.

"Elite Prospects - NHL PIM Stats 2008-09." Elite Prospects, 2019.

"Elite Prospects - Yannick Turcotte." Elite Prospects, 2019.

CHAPTER 17: PLAYERS TO LOOK OUT FOR IN THE 2019–20 ECHL SEASON

"2018-19 Regular Season Standings." Echl.Com. 2019.

"Elite Prospects - 2019-20 Toledo Walleye." Elite Prospects, 2019.

"Elite Prospects - 2018-19 Shawinigan Cataractes." Elite Prospects, 2019.

"Elite Prospects - Alan Lyszczarczyk." Elite Prospects, 2019.

"Elite Prospects - Alexis D'Aoust." Elite Prospects, 2019.

"Elite Prospects - Cameron Askew." Elite Prospects, 2019.

"Elite Prospects - Charle-Edouard D'Astous." Elite Prospects, 2019.

"Elite Prospects - Cole Cassels." Elite Prospects, 2019.

"Elite Prospects - Colton Point." Elite Prospects, 2019.

"Elite Prospects - Dante Hannoun." Elite Prospects, 2019.

"Elite Prospects - Dylan Sadowy." Elite Prospects, 2019.

"Elite Prospects - François Beauchemin." Elite Prospects, 2019.

"Elite Prospects - Gabriel Gagné." Elite Prospects, 2019.

"Elite Prospects - Giorgio Estephan." Elite Prospects, 2019.

"Elite Prospects - Hayden Hawkey." Elite Prospects, 2019.

"Elite Prospects - Keeghan Howdeshell." Elite Prospects, 2019.

"Elite Prospects - Keoni Texeira." Elite Prospects, 2019.

"Elite Prospects - Kirill Ustimenko." Elite Prospects, 2019.

"Elite Prospects - Jan Drozg." Elite Prospects, 2019.

"Elite Prospects - Jakub Skarek." Elite Prospects, 2019.

"Elite Prospects - Jesse Schultz." Elite Prospects, 2019.

"Elite Prospects - Ken Appleby." Elite Prospects, 2019.

"Elite Prospects - Patrick Bajkov." Elite Prospects, 2019.

"Elite Prospects - Robby Jackson." Elite Prospects, 2019.

"Elite Prospects - Travis Barron." Elite Prospects, 2019.

"Elite Prospects - Ty Ronning." Elite Prospects, 2019.